Maw Broon's Afternoon Tea Book

Written by Maw with the
help and advice of
The Glebe Street Afternoon
Tea Ladies

Recipes by Gilda T Smith

(Tea)

Tee hee!

Written up neatly by Miss Gardner
Stapled together by Bella Frame
Drawings by Annie Todd
Copied on the fly on the photostat machine
at work by Ella Brownlee

Waverley Books

What STARTS WITH a T, ends WITH T, and is filled WITH T? A TeapoT.

by Ae Twin

Ane o' the unwritten rules o' The Glebe Street Afternoon Tea Ladies group is:

"aye keep yer hats on".

Maw x

Contents

Mind Your Teas and Qs or
The Etiquette of Afternoon Tea

The Recipes

Dainty Savouries and Sandwiches

Cakes and Sweet Pastries

Scones, Teabreads and Biscuits

Mind Your
Teas and Qs
or
The Etiquette of
Afternoon Tea

<u>Rules for the Monthly "At Home"</u>

At each "At Home", the host of the next month's meeting will be appointed.

In order to ensure that the host of our next "at home" has enough chairs etc., applications to take part must be made to Mrs Broon (i.e. Maw Broon) three weeks in advance.

The appointed host will prepare a selection of sandwiches, scones and tea and coffee (usually for about 15 people).

The attendees will all bring several of one kind of small cake or dainty savoury of their choice, to be shared by all attendees.

When making the application to attend, in writing or by phone (Maw doesn't do email yet), please inform Mrs Broon of what you'll be bringing. <u>Nae bought-cakes allowed.</u>

Mrs Broon will make the list of attendees. (In the event of duplication of baking Maw will suggest you make something else of her choosing.)

Maw will provide everyone with directions to the host's house.

There is a rota for those who will assist the host on the morning of the meeting (and help with all the dishes after).

The Etiquette of Afternoon Tea

The members o' oor group, The Glebe Street Afternoon Tea Ladies, hae ta'en it in turns tae hae monthly "At Homes" wi' ane anither for decades. During these get-togethers we share new recipes, taste each ither's baking and *politely* put the world tae rights. There are some strong personalities and opinions amongst us but we've managed ower the years tae ~~never rarely~~ hardly ever fall oot, and tae enjoy each ither's cakes and company by following a few simple rules.

We share oor experience wi' you here in this wee book. We'll gie you enough recipes and advice tae haud your ain efternoon tea, safe in the knowledge that you havenae committed any social or culinary faux pas (that's a "rid neck" for those who dinnae ken French, unlike masel').

Manners

You can get ower fashed aboot etiquette. Etiquette can be bamboozling if you're no' "in the know". And that, when you come doon tae it, is the point o' etiquette: it shows up those who are in the know and those who are no' in the know – which is no' an awfy nice thing really.

Which fork do you use, how do you eat your scone, whit tea plate is yours, etc? Dinnae worry ower much aboot that the noo, we'll explain aboot the right things tae dae as we go along and by the end o' this you'll be able tae share a scone wi" royalty withoot embarrassing yersel'.

Manners are anither matter though. They're mair important, at least in the opinion o' The Glebe Street Afternoon Tea Ladies. And manners are often just a matter o' common sense. They're aboot being respectful tae others (no' aboot what bit o' cutlery tae use). For example, fowk's ears dinna need tae be offended by slittering and slavvering, and their eyes dinna need tae see the contents o' your mooth as ye try tae talk wi' a moothful o' scone. If there is only one eclair left, be sure tae offer it tae your companions first, thus: "Ye'll no' be wantin' that last eclair will ye?"

Some o' the niceties o' the rules o' efternoon tea are no' as obvious as these but, even so, <u>maist o' them</u> were thought up for good, sensible reasons.

Feedin' time at Glebe Street

What is Afternoon Tea?

In Britain, when Queen Victoria was just a lassie, efternoon tea started off as being a wee meal, eaten around 3 pm, tae keep you going efter yer denner* until your proper tea.* Ower the years it grew intae a mair grand, three-course cairry-on and has now become a bit o' an institution in Britain and Ireland. The English, Scots, Welsh and Irish might hae their differences frae time tae time but, while we're arguing, we'll never say no tae a wee cuppa tea and a bit o' cake: "Oh, a wee scone, dinna mind if I do. Now, what was that you were saying aboot Culloden, Marjorie?"

There are a number o' rules aboot how efternoon tea should be served. Some rules might

*Translation:–
lunch — yer denner
dinner — yer tea

The Etiquette of Afternoon Tea

seem a bitty daft. Miss Gardner, frae oor group (she's the teacher), says most fowk like boundaries an' rules, even though they might no' think they do. Efternoon tea is a ritual, and the rules you follow tae carry it oot help tae mak' it feel like a real occasion. Dinna get a' fashed aboot it though, ye're meant tae enjoy it.

A'thing aboot the way you serve efternoon tea should say "genteel". It should be presented in a bonnie way, on the nicest crockery you own, and made wi" good quality loose tea served frae china teapots intae china teacups wi" saucers (never mugs or beakers). The cakes are dainty, the sandwiches are presented in fingers or triangles, wi" the crusts ta'en aff.

It's aboot impressing fowk, nae doubt aboot that. This started aff as a bit o' snobbery: in later Victorian times, efternoon teas had become a chance for well-tae-do ladies tae socialise, and climb the social ladder ... awfy pan-loafy.

But no' in Glebe Street. For oor group it's no' aboot climbing ony ladders (just the kitchen steps tae reach the big platters). Sure, ye'll impress yer pals wi" how guid your scones are and how tidy your hoose is and all that – so it _is_ aboot showing aff. But ye're also saying tae fowk: "I like you, you're worth the hassle o' me pressing my good tablecloth and polishing the silver."

The Meenister gate-crashed again!

What Afternoon Tea is NOT

It's no' a buffet. It's a sit-doon tea. Everyone needs a seat next tae a table rather than sitting wi" their plate on their knee.

It's no' "high tea". A typical high tea will be a hot meal, like fish an' chips an' peas, served wi" bread an' butter an' a mug o' tea, an' followed by a cream bun or similar cake. This is served at around 5 or 6 o'clock as an efter-work or efter-school meal.

It's no' a boozy pairty (although Agnes Arbuckle does like a wee sherry). Many places will serve Champagne wi" efternoon tea. It is the opinion o' The Glebe Street Afternoon Tea Ladies that fizzy wine disnae go wi" sweet cakes. The best Assam tea goes wi" cake. The Glebe Street Afternoon Tea Ladies dinna drink wine in the efternoon. Try <u>The Church Street Afternoon Tea Ladies</u> if you want that kind o' cairry-on.

Paw Broon's interpretation of high tea

The Presentation

Efternoon tea is available a' place these days, and it maistly aye looks the same. A three-tier cake stand is the norm. And nice china.

At home

Now, when serving efternoon tea at home, a cake stand isnae necessary. It's nice but you dinna need it. Presenting your cakes in a neat and bonnie way is much mair important. This can be done by simply laying the food oot on bonnie plates (they dinna even have tae be matching, mis-matched is a' the rage these days) on starched, pressed linen tablecloths.

Favourite Recipes

19

3 egg whites
5 oz/150 g caster sugar
Red food colouring paste
or powder
Brown food colouring paste
or powder

Coffee essence
Raspberry syrup
Vanilla essence
Pink sugar sprinkles

Whisk egg whites in a glass bowl till soft peaks. Add the sugar gradually and whisk till thick and glossy with stiff peaks. Divide into three. Colour the first with red, the second with brown and leave the third white. Put into separate piping bags, each with a jagged nozzle, and pipe into swirls. Sprinkle with pink sugar. Bake in a cool oven (110–140°C) for about an hour then turn off and leave overnight. Sandwich together with cream, flavoured with raspberry, vanilla or coffee.

Meringue Whirls

In the tea room

In a tea room or café, the three-tier cake stand saves a lot o' space and fowk seem tae like it – it creates a bit o' a spectacle. Watch the fowk who've ordered efternoon tea. When their three tiers arrive they usually make an "ooooh" noise or giggle away tae themselves like dafties. It's an occasion.

It wisna much o' an occasion in this posh hotel, the wee tearoom would hae been better

The cake stand

The sandwiches and dainty savouries are usually presented on the bottom tier. (Some tearooms may put these in the middle section. We think because you tend tae eat the savouries first, you should put them on the bottom o' the cake stand. There will, nae doubt, be those who disagree [such as The Auchentogle Cake Ladies], but aren't there always! It's like politics!)

The Etiquette of Afternoon Tea

The second tier has the wee cakes such as tarts, meringues, wee sponges and cream cakes. On the top tier you present the scones (uncut, and freshly made that morning, wi" portions o' butter, cream and jam in wee bowls), pancakes and teabreads. Maybe a wee biscuit. Sometimes you'll see something a wee bitty different on this top tier, like a wee portion o' posset, jelly or trifle, and this can look bonnie but it's no' traditional. The top tier used tae be for the warm foods, and some drawings in old books show a domed cover for this.

For oor get-togethers wi" a' the ladies it's no' practical tae serve warm items. It's hard enough making 15–20 perfect scones and enough roonds o' sandwiches for everyone that very morning withoot trying tae mak' sure the scones and tea cakes are kept roasty toasty hot. A' oor cakes are at room temperature except for cream cakes which are, of course, chilled. (Dinna dae what Jessie Coulter did an' leave them ootside on the window ledge tae stay cool. Seagulls, ye understand!)

The Etiquette of Scones

Noo, scones are a must for efternoon tea, though I'm telt they werena even in it till the 20th century (that's efter Queen Victoria died – I wonder if she had something against scones?). We cannae imagine efternoon tea withoot them. Scones taste best when they're freshest so the Glebe Street ladies try tae mak' them the morning o' oor meetings.

Ane o' the rules o' serving scones at efternoon tea is that they should be whole, rather than cut in twa, and certainly no' already spread wi" cream an' jam. The reason for this? Well, it _probably_ keeps the scones fresher and it also gives fowk the option o' spreading them wi" whatever they prefer*.

Fruit scones are traditionally served wi" butter only; plain scones wi" butter and jam, or cream and jam. Naebody is going tae arrest you if you put

*Jessie pits on enough jam for fower folk!

28

Whit happens to a scone when you've eaten it? It's scone! by ither twin

jam on a fruit scone, though Lizzie Gow will "tut".
Sometimes "tut, TUT!"

No' splitting them up before serving means
leftover scones (though rare) will keep better and can
be pinched by bairns and menfolk at (high) tea time.
In some circles it is genteel tae tear the scone up
and eat in wee pieces. Perhaps if one's scones are
on the ginormous side it might be unseemly tae lift
a whole muckle ane tae one's mooth. That might be
the case, but NEVER dip the bits o' scone in the
jam or cream pots. Broon Twins tak' note.

The Correct Equipment

Teapot (or pots)

Coffee pot (or pots)

China cups, saucers and tea plates. (They dinna a' have tae be matching. But nae cracked anes or cups wi" shoogly handles.)

Tea strainer and bowl

Cutlery: (one each o') butter knives, cake forks, teaspoons (silver if ye hae them)

Linen napkins and linen tablecloths

Pots for hot water

Cream and milk jugs

Sugar bowls

Sugar tongs (for cubes) *

Plate for lemon slices and bowl for discarded slices.

* Now that's posh!

How to Lay the Table

Each table must be covered wi" a tablecloth. Starched white linen is the very dab for a formal do, but I've seen some lassies just use some nice patterned bits o' material. Decorate each table wi" a wee arrangement o' flooers. (If you've lots o' tables and no' lots o' vases, used tin cans or jeely jars, washed oot thoroughly, can make braw wee vases for flooers. Tie ribbons round them. Cut the flooer stems short.)

Place a tea plate in the centre o' each setting and place the saucer and tea cup on top. Napkin tae the left side o' the tea plate setting. Closed edge o' the napkin tae the left and the open edge tae the right. Place a butter knife tae the right o' the plate, a cake fork tae the right o' the knife and a teaspoon on the saucer. Napkin rings are no' needed. (They winna fit folded napkins onyway!)

Tae save space, we sometimes put the cutlery on top o' the napkin, tae the right o' the plate.

In a fancy tea room you might hae a bread plate and a luncheon plate. It's no' practical tae fit that much crockery on the table if you just hae a wee sitting room an' a few occasional tables.

if an occasional Table is occasionally a Table is iT also occasionally a chaiR?

Common sense an' neatness must win ower daft rules sometimes!

If it's a cream tea, have enough reachable pots o' cream and jam for everyone and plenty serving spoons.

Ensure cream, milk, sugar and lemon slices are accessible at each table.

The hostess will keep refilling cups and removing any waste.

Pots o' coffee and tea won't be left on the table for guests tae help themselves. This way the hostess

can be sure that a'body is getting a full cup o' tea
and no' sitting wi" an empty cup.

Mrs Smythe wants it noted
that she disapproves of this
setting — it's no' fancy
enough — and she will always
put oot the full complement of
proper efternoon teaware.
So there ye go!

Anither showin' up!

Add the rule: No mobile phones
allowed at the table. Yon Jenny
Smith is aye textin her man —or
somebody else's man, some say ...

The Art of Tea

Scald the teapot and empty it, then put the tea in, allowing one teaspoonful for each person with an extra one "for the pot". Pour over it as much boiling water as will cover the tea completely. Let it infuse for three minutes.

Fill up the pot with boiling water and use immediately. Soft water is the best, and should be freshly boiled, because water that has been boiled several times will not draw the strength of the tea properly. Some teapots are now fitted with a perforated cup to contain the tea leaves and enable them to be removed after infusion. Otherwise use a tea strainer.

Serve in fine China; this has a pleasant and genteel feel to the mouth. Add milk and sugar after the tea has been poured.

How to Make Tea

Water must be fresh. No' boiled and cooled several times. The best water is at the But an' Ben but we dinna hae tea parties there. Maybe we should!

Water must be freshly boiled then immediately poured ower the tea leaves. Boilin' water releases the flavour frae the leaves, tepid water disnae. The teapot must be scalded afore adding the boilin' water for tea (so that the pot is warmed and the boilin' water doesn't lose any heat).

Loose tea has a better flavour than tea bags. The reason is that the leaves hae mair room tae move and the tea brews quicker (staying hotter). And ye'd be asked tae leave oor club if ye ever got caught using tea bags onyway!

Paw trying some of thon Lapsang Souchong

But Grawpaw loves it — says it's like Islay malt, Hen

How to Drink Tea

Stir your tea demurely in your cup, nae need tae make a wee tinkling sound. Once you've finished stirring your tea in the cup tak' the teaspoon oot and leave in your saucer. Nae need for a wee "ting ting" on the side o' the cup wi' the spoon efter you've stirred. You're no' in an orchestra.

Nae need tae put milk in first tae prevent the cup cracking. Ower-fragile china might hae needed it in the old days. But tea is never richt at boilin' point when it's poured frae a teapot into a cup. It's aye better tae see the strength o' the brew afore the milk goes in.

Dinna wave or point wi" your cup in your hand. It's rude and you'll spill it.

Dinna blow on your hot tea tae cool it or waft it wi" your bunnet. No' that ony o' oor ladies wear bunnets. Hats, aye. On no account pour it intae your saucer. (Ye can dae that when ye're on yer own.)

Those who like black tea may also like a slice o' lemon. Some o' the mair strongly fragranced teas such as Earl Grey and *Ah dinna like them* Lapsang Souchong are probably better withoot anything in them at a' but some may ask for lemon. *or a sweetie to tak' the taste awa', Maw*

Place thin slices o' lemon on a plate by the milk and sugar and provide tongs, a fork or even some cocktail sticks tae lift the slices delicately into the tea.

The lemon slice goes in the cup efter pouring the tea. Dinna poke it wi' your spoon tae get mair lemon juice oot o' it. Dinna fish oot a squashed lemon slice and stick it in your saucer either, it'll mak' drips. The hostess should have provided a bowl on the table for waste such as old lemon slices which she should remove, empty and replace regularly. Dinna stick your pinkies oot (page 45).

The rare occasion o'
Paw Broon makin' the tea
withoot being asked twice.

Tea Varieties

Assam tea has a rare colour, strength and flavour. Strong withoot being bitter and withoot having tae brew ower long. It's usually the kind they use as the main ingredient in English Breakfast Tea blends. Like Joe Broon, it's a guid all-rounder.

It's nice wi" milk and withoot – and it's the tea o' choice for The Glebe Street Afternoon Tea Ladies.

Another ane that makes it into the breakfast blends is Keemun tea, an English spelling o' Qimen, a county in Anhui (Anhwei) province, China. So now ye ken!

Darjeeling tea is mair light and floral. It's awfy nice. I like it black and brewed a wee bit longer. Paw likes it wi" milk and fower sugars.

Kenya tea is quick brewing and strong wi" a wee hint o' lemon.

Ceylon (the auld name for Sri Lanka) tea is deep gold in colour and has a citrussy taste.

It's no' my cup o' tea

Scented teas, best served without milk:

Earl Grey has a braw orange scent because it's flavoured wi' oil frae the bergamot orange. A few o' oor group just love it. It reminds me a bit o' suntan lotion (in a good way).

Lady Grey smells o' tangerines. (I dinna ken if thae twa were winchin' or no'.)

Milk in first or no'?

Reminds me o' the smell of Granpaw's pipe while he creosotes his shed.

Lapsang souchong has an awfy smoky flavour. Betty Pringle serves it when she has her efternoons, and I think it's dear tae buy.

Rose pouchong is a braw rose-scented strong black China tea. It's no' cheap either. If you're on a diet and fancy a Turkish Delight, have a cup o' this instead. You'll still want a Turkish Delight but you'll be less thirsty! Ha ha. It goes really well wi' cake and I think it's best served withoot milk.

PLANTS USED AS FOOD

TEA,
thea viridis.

PLATE XVII.

Green's Tea

Pesented with Wills full strength

Other Beverages

Herbal and fruit teas

Well, they're no' really tea are they? Peppermint and ginger are good tae keep in the hoose in case anyone has indigestion. There are a lot o' flavours going on at efternoon tea, so it might be best tae keep fruit and herbal teas for another time. However, some o' your guests might want tae steer clear o' caffeine if their nerves are bad.

Caffeine-free "teas"

their nerves micht be an awfy lot worse efter an efternoon wi the Tea Ladies! frae Hen

Nettle tea is a surprisingly nice brew wi" a mild, sweet flavour that will go nicely wi" cake. Camomile is mair fragrant but still goes well wi" a wee fruit scone ... and jam.

Rooibos is a caffeine-free "tea" actually made from bark. It has a strong colour and flavour that's meant tae be similar tae tea.

It's no' for me. I need my real tea. It's like barking up the wrong tea! 43

Coffee

Coffee at an efternoon tea? Michty me! Coffee can be made in a cafetière and be served straight frae that, or it can be made in ae pot and strained into anither and, unlike loose leaf tea, it's best made wi water that is just aff the boil. Coffee goes bitter if boiled. Serve wi" cream.

You get a fancy thing ca'ed a moka pot, whaur the water bubbles up through the coffee grounds and makes braw strong coffee (nearly as strong as the espresso you get in the Italiano shops). Serve in wee cups or your coffee drinkers will get up-tae-high-doh wi" caffeine.

I cringe when I see fowk stickin' their pinkies oot tryin' tae be posh. So does Sadie Wilson. She lost her pinkie in the co-op bacon slicer in 1953.

frae Joe

Behaviour at Table

Pinkies in or oot?

Sticking your pinkie oot when you drink frae a teacup might help you balance your tea cup if the handle is awfy wee, or if you're drinking frae a wee Chinese bowl. However, in Glebe Street we're no' drinking oot o' wee Chinese bowls, and the cups hae perfectly guid handles. Your cup is probably perfectly well balanced withoot sticking a pinkie oot, and you'll probably just look like you're trying ower hard tae be fancy. Pinkies in, boys an' girls!

Here we are — trying ower hard tae be fancy

Napkins

If you've tae leave the table, put your napkin back on the table, tae the left o' your plate (no' on your plate). Some fowk say you should put your napkin on the chair. Here's why no': yon Bessie Briggs put a big jam-stained napkin on my upholstered chair. Ruined! You can wash a tablecloth, so napkins on the table it is! Or ye micht no' get invited back. Dinna tuck your napkin into your collar. Fowk that are awfy slavvery might be tempted tae do this.

Your napkin's no' a bib. You are adults. Well, adult-ish. The trick is tae try no' tae be a slavver. Eat in a genteel manner wi" wee bits o' cake rather than ramming big dods into your mooth as quickly as you can.

An' sip your tea. Dinna gulp it doon tae try an' dislodge the muckle bit o' cake that has got stuck in your greedy thrapple.

Elbows

Never rest your elbows on the table, it looks slouchy and rude and we're meant tae be having a wee occasion, no' a wee rest.

Handbags

Dinna sit your handbag on the table. Handbags sit on floors and they might hae germs on them.

In Summary

Efternoon Tea should be an enjoyable thing, and it only needs tae be as formal as you want it tae be – but mak' sure it's still an occasion.

We dinna hae enough occasions in this life!

Enjoy yersels!

The bairns look well behaved here — must be fu' o cake

Favourite Recipes

17

2 ¾ cups/12 ¾ oz/380 g
  flour
⅓ tsp salt
1 tsp ground ginger
1 egg
3 tsps baking powder
⅔ cup 8 oz/240 g syrup

⅓ cup/2 ½ oz/75 g brown
  sugar
⅓ cup/2 ½ oz/75 g melted
  butter
Currants (optional)
Royal icing (optional)

Sift the flour, baking powder, salt and ginger together. Mix the sugar, syrup, egg and melted butter together, and add the dry ingredients to make a soft dough. Cut into the shape of little men.

Bake in a moderate oven (180°C) for 12 minutes. Make eyes, nose and mouth with currants, or ice the features on afterwards with royal icing of the correct consistency.

Gingerbread Men

Favourite Recipes

14

8 egg whites
1 cup/7 oz/210 g sugar
½ tsp cream of tartar

1 cup/5 oz/150 g flour
1 tsp vanilla

A fatless sponge. Beat egg white till foaming, add cream of tartar and beat till stiff. Beat in the sugar gradually using a wooden spoon. Add vanilla. Fold in the flour. Bake in a round

tin (8 inch) in a hot oven (190-200°C) for around 30-50 minutes.

Serve with whipped cream and jam to ruin the fat-free title!

Angel Cake

Favourite

15

A use for all the egg yolks not used in the Angel Cake

⅓ cup/2 ½ oz/75 g butter
1 tsp vanilla
2 cups/10 oz/300 g flour
1 cup/7 oz/210g sugar

8 egg yolks
3 tsps baking powder
½ teaspoon salt

Cream the butter and sugar. Beat the egg yolks till light, fluffy and yellow. Add to the mixture. Sift dry ingredients and fold in. Add a little milk

if required. Add vanilla. Bake for 45 minutes at 180°C in an 8-inch tin, or two sandwich tins.

Gold Cake

The Recipes

Bread You Can Make At Home

1.—Take 3½ lb. flour, 1 oz. compressed yeast, 1 teaspoonful sugar, 2 teaspoonfuls salt, and 2 pints lukewarm water. Sieve the flour and salt into a large basin and warm them in a cool oven, as this helps the bread to rise. Cream the yeast and sugar in a small basin, add half the water, and mix well together.

2.—Make a well in the centre of the warm flour and strain in the yeast and water. Stir in enough flour to form a thick, smooth batter, leaving a wall of flour round the edges. Sprinkle the surface with flour, cover the basin with a cloth, and set in a warm place till the batter is covered with bubbles.

3.—Mix in the rest of the flour gradually, adding the rest of the water until a soft dough is formed. Dough to be baked in tins should be left soft, but dough that is to be baked in fancy shapes must be a little firmer. Turn the dough on to a floured board and knead for 15 minutes. Then return it to a floured basin cover, and let stand for one hour.

4.—Next turn the dough on to the floured board again and re-knead lightly. To make a Cottage Loaf make one large ball and place a smaller ball on top. Press a floured finger through the middle of both and make four cuts at regular intervals round the sides. Place the loaf on a baking sheet and let it stand for 15 minutes to rise Then bake for 1½ hours.

5.—If the dough is to be baked in a tin, grease the tin first and carefully put in the dough, allowing it to sink until the tin is only half full. Then set the tin in a warm place and let the dough rise for 15 minutes before baking it in a moderate oven for 1¼ hours. Have the oven hot to begin with, but lower the heat when the bread is slightly browned.

6.—The bread is ready when it gives a hollow sound when tapped on the bottom. Whenever the bread is taken from the oven turn it on its side on a wire tray to allow the steam to escape. When quite cold the bread should be stored in a ventilated tin in a cool, dry place. If it is to be kept wrap it in greaseproof paper, then in a cloth before storing.

Dainty Savouries
and Sandwiches

Should Victoria
sandwich no' be
in This
Section?

Sandwich Making

What kind of bread?

Choose firm, fresh bread (no' ower soft, no' ower dry and crumbly). Try the medium-sliced supermarket own-brand. I've found them tae be nice and thinly cut, wi' a good number o' slices per loaf and the bread is a firmer consistency than some fancier, softer breads. Choose thin-sliced bread, or cut as thin as you can if you're cutting your ain (guid bakeries can cut your loaf for you).

How many?

An average sliced loaf has aboot 20 slices in it. You'll need approximately 150 g butter, softened, tae spread on the bread. So that's 10 uncut sandwiches frae a loaf and 40 quarters or fingers. Estimate fower quarters/fingers per guest. However, you know your guests best. Some fowk always need mair. Be sure tae have enough for a'body. It's a poor show no' tae put oot enough pieces ... sorry, sandwiches.

Spreading

Spread a' the slices o' bread right tae the edge wi' softened butter. Beat the butter using an electric whisk until light and fluffy. This makes the butter easier tae spread and it goes further. Cheaper!

A guid coating o' butter stops the bread getting soggy frae any ower-moist fillings.

Spread fillings evenly ower half the slices, top wi" the rest o' the slices and press doon lightly. Place on a baking tray and cover wi" a clean, damp tea towel (no' wet, wring it oot firmly), cover tightly wi" cling film and chill for an hour until firm. After chilling, trim off the crusts and cut in the way you prefer. I admit, I feel bad cutting the crusts aff. I always tell the bairns tae eat theirs so they can get curly hair.

We haTe cURLY haiR and cRUSTS

Cutting

Use a long, awfy sharp knife tae cut the crusts aff and for cutting the sandwiches.

After each cut, clean the knife wi" a clean damp cloth tae produce neat sandwiches.

Always wipe your knife
with the sharp edge
away from your hand.

Triangles

Displaying yer sandwiches as triangles is no' being ower fancy. Wi" the sandwiches lined up sitting on their bottom edges wi" pointed ends sticking up, it's easier tae see what the filling is (and so you avoid guests liftin' up the sandwiches tae see what they are and then puttin' them back, the worse for wear: "naw ... I dinna like corned beef ... now, whit's in 'at ane?").

Fingers

We dinna like The sound o' eaTin' fingeRs

This is a bonnie way o' showing sandwiches on a cake stand. Once the sandwich is spread and chilled as on the previous page, cut aff the crusts and cut each sandwich into four fingers lengthways.

Pinwheels

Trim the crusts frae slices o' a sandwich loaf, flatten slightly using a rolling pin (roll only once or twice). Spread all slices wi" softened butter then spread again wi" your chosen filling (mak' it a smooth filling). Roll up, then wrap each roll tightly wi" cling film and chill for an hour. Trim each end and then cut into slices like a Swiss roll.

These are quid for bairns' parties too

Club sandwiches

This is a sandwich wi" three slices o' bread in it. Butter your middle slice o' bread on both sides, and the top and bottom slices on one side. Build up your sandwich wi" a filling between each layer. Press together firmly. Cover and chill as before then trim crusts and cut into the required size.

Neapolitan sandwiches

Make as club sandwiches but use three contrasting breads, and two contrasting but complementary fillings.

A picnic is al-fresco efternoon tea

Sandwich Fillings

Avoid any ower-wet fillings. Tomatoes need seeds removed, and cucumber will be less wet wi" seeds scooped oot too.

Try no' tae use ower-strong flavours such as raw garlic and raw onion. Some fowk really like it but when you're catering for a big group you're better tae be a bit mair subtle. Spring onions and chives can gie a mair mellow flavour that will appeal tae mair fowk. Herbs like coriander are no' some fowk's cuppa tea – avoid unless everyone loves it. Low-fat mayonnaise is a great invention and can be substituted in any o' these fillings withoot anyone really noticing. Watch oot if choosing low-fat cheeses though – they can be a bit tasteless sometimes.

Cucumber

This is THE traditional efternoon tea sandwich. Peel the skin frae the cucumber. Cut in half lengthways and scoop oot the seeds. Cut paper-thin slices wi' a mandolin cutter (or the tattie peeler). Sprinkle wi' salt and leave it for aboot 20 minutes. (Salt draws oot moisture that might make your sandwiches ower soggy.) Enough time tae spread your bread and put the kettle on. Spread white bread wi' lightly salted butter, right up tae the edges. Pat the salted cucumber slices wi' kitchen roll or a clean tea towel tae tak' oot moisture, and place on the buttered bread. Dinna add onions or garlic or mint or vinegar or pepper or glitter – just butter and cucumber and salt on nice bread. Cut the crusts aff and cut into fingers or triangles. Richt posh!

Chicken

Coronation chicken

To 500 g cooked, cold chicken add aboot 4 or 5 tablespoons o' mayonnaise, a tablespoon o' mango chutney and a teaspoon o' curry powder. Taste and add salt and pepper if required. A wee bit o' crunch is nice in it: such as a finely chopped apple (soaked in lemon juice), or finely chopped celery, or some flaked almonds.

I think if I'd just been made Queen I'd be a wee bitty disappointed if it was just pieces for my tea. (Does the Queen even ken whit a "piece" is?

62

More chicken fillings

Tae ensure the filling is no' going tae fall oot - if only it was as easy tae stop your guests falling oot - you could combine chopped chicken wi" cream cheese, mayonnaise, etc. A few ideas:

Chicken and sweetcorn in mayonnaise.

Chicken and cranberry sauce.

Chicken, celery, grapes, and spring onions wi" cream cheese.

Chicken and avocado (as guacamole, below).

Guacamole

Guacamole is easy but put lime or lemon juice in it tae stop it going broon. Dice a seeded tomato awfy finely. Chop some spring onions. Halve and scoop oot the insides o' an avocado. Mash wi" a tattie champer. Add the tomatoes, onions, salt and white pepper.

Truth be told, the Tea Ladies are no' great fans o' guacamole. Corned beef is mair their thing.

Egg mayonnaise

Chop up some biled eggs (ane for every twa fowk), add seasoning and enough mayonnaise tae bind it together (no' ower sloppy). Ye can add chopped parsley; mustard cress; curry powder; smoked paprika; chilli flakes; chopped tomatoes (cherry toms are best as the skin o' the flesh is already thin). You could also sieve the biled eggs and mix up wi" chopped chives and cream.

Cream cheese

Cream cheese makes a great base for fillings as it has a subtle flavour that can combine wi" just aboot anything. Layer the cheese wi" chutney or pickle, smoked salmon, cooked ham, sardines. Mix wi" flaked smoked haddock, chopped tomato (seeds removed), chopped cucumber (skinned and seeds removed), grated cheese and spring onion. But no' a' at once!

Cooked meats gRanpaW is an old ham

Cooked ham is nice wi" English mustard, mayonnaise, sliced tomato or chutney. Dinna add ower-many salad ingredients or the sandwiches might fall apart. Roast beef is good wi" English mustard or horseradish sauce or just by itself. Corned beef and tomato. Cut tomato in half and scoop oot the seeds. Cut up finely and mash wi" a tin or slices o' corned beef. Season wi" salt and pepper. Delicious!

Smoked salmon

Smoked salmon can be served on its own or wi" cream cheese. You could add thinly sliced, skinned, seeded cucumber too. Dinna add ower-many ither ingredients tae a smoked salmon filling – it's best kept simple wi a wee drappie lemon juice squeezed ower it and some black pepper.

This is no' for me.
Ah like ma fish cooked

66

Cheddar cheese

Thinly sliced, no' grated – or it will escape! Nice wi" chutney or pickle. Make cheese savoury spread by mixing grated cheese wi" mayonnaise (or cream cheese) and chives. Guid for spreading on pinwheel sandwiches (page 58).

Tuna

Tuna and sweetcorn: Drain a tin o' tuna (the steak, not the flakes), and shred the flesh wi" a fork. Then mix in a few tablespoons o' mayonnaise and a wee drappie finely chopped spring onions or red onions. Add tinned, drained sweetcorn. Season well (probably just pepper, shouldnae need salt).

Tuna and cucumber: Drain one tin o' tuna. Shred wi" a fork. Chop a 3-inch wedge o' skinned cucumber in half lengthways and scoop oot the seeds. Combine wi" the tuna and a few tablespoons o' mayonnaise. Season well.

Prawn mayonnaise

Mix cooked, chilled, wee prawns wi" enough mayonnaise tae bind them together, and season using a wee bitty white pepper. Or add tae that a skoosh o' tomato ketchup, a squeeze o' lemon, a shake o' paprika and finely chopped spring onions.

Sweet fillings

Try some o' these suggestions chopped and mixed wi" cream cheese: drained chopped pineapple, chopped peach, grated apple and chopped dates, grated apple wi" chopped celery and chopped dates, chopped preserved ginger.

Adding chopped ginger tae some o' the ither combinations might be nice – for example, chopped pineapple.

Mix a' grated apple fillings wi" a wee bitty lemon juice tae help prevent it going broon.

Banana: Mash two bananas (braw fun – get the bairns tae dae it) and add the juice o' half a lemon. Cream together 50 g o' butter and 50 g sugar. Mix well wi" the banana.

Particularly nice on broon bread. This would make an awfy bonnie pinwheel.

bUT a disappoinTing spaRe wheel

Nº 19

MACDUFF'S

SCOTTISH FOODS OF QUALITY

Ingredients:
1 kg rhubarb
1 kg sugar
Juice 1 lemon

Method:
Wipe the rhubarb and cut in 2 cm lengths. Put in glass or stainless steel bowl with the sugar sprinkled on in layers. Add the lemon juice. Cover and leave overnight. Put in preserving pan and bring to boil. Boil rapidly till thick. Skim, cool and stir before potting in sterilised jars. Cover with circles of greaseproof paper and jar lids while still warm.

Rhubarb Jam

Dainty Savouries

Now there are two important things tae bear in mind regarding dainty savouries: 1 – they need tae be dainty, 2 – they need tae be savoury. Just ma wee joke.

You're maist likely serving them cauld, and cauld things need tae be mair strongly flavoured than hot things. There'll be a scientific reason for this but I dinna ken it. Anyway, season them well. I avoid anything ower garlicky but that's a personal preference for no' wanting tae smell garlicky breath aff o' fowk.

It's nice if they are edible (isn't it always?) in ane or twa bites. They are going tae look awfy bonnie on your cake stand if they do look wee or bite-sized, rather than like a muckle big Forfar bridie or a Scotch pie!

This is incorrect. The plural is vols—au—vent no' vol—au—vents. It's french for "flight in the wind",

Horace

Vol-au-Vents

HoRace is full o wind

This is a long recipe — we've tried tae keep things short an' sweet in this book for the maist part — but once ye ken how tae mak' puff pastry ye can use it for loads o' ither stuff.

Puff pastry:

(Annie's done a wee drawing on page 75 tae help.)

  250 g plain flour (strong flour is best)

  100 g fat (butter, lard or shortening)

  Pinch salt

  150 ml cold water

  Juice of half a lemon

  150 g butter

We made puff pastry by blowing the crumbs aff the table

Fillings:

  Chicken wi" sweetcorn and red pepper

  Fried mushrooms and fresh tarragon

  Chopped cooked ham wi" grainy mustard

White sauce:

Make a white sauce o' a coating consistency (a bit thicker than pouring consistency).

  50 g butter

  50 g flour

  500 ml milk

  Salt and white pepper

Pastry method:

Add the salt to the flour and rub in aboot 100 g o' fat. You can substitute lard or shortening for this amount o' fat as it gies a good texture tae the pastry. (Dinna be tempted tae use self-raising flour, the texture will turn oot a' wrang.)

Add the juice o' half a lemon tae the flour and fat mixture. Gradually add the water, just a wee bit at a time, tae the flour and mix the dough tae an elastic consistency. (Remember you can add mair liquid but you cannae take it oot!)

Turn oot the dough onto your work surface (no need tae flour it yet), and work it until it's smooth. Make into a round, cut a cross in it (like the top o' a baked potato, see fig. 1) and ease oot the corners created by the cross just a wee bit tae create four "ears". Wrap in cling film and let it rest in the fridge for at least an hour (an overnight rest is better if you've the time).

When ready tae roll the dough, first soften the 150 g butter a wee bit by hitting it – in a plastic bag or between two pieces o' greaseproof paper – wi" a rolling pin till it's softened but still cold from the fridge. As a guide, it should end up the same consistency as the dough. Then make the butter into a square shape.

Flour your surface lightly and roll dough into a cross shape by rolling on each o' the "ears" you made (see fig. 2). Make the dough four times thicker in the middle o' the cross than the outsides. Put the softened, square pat o' butter into the centre (see fig. 3) and fold the four sides o' the dough evenly over the butter, sealing it in and leaving no gaps (see fig. 4). You dinna want any butter poking through.

Press lightly and roll into a long rectangle. Watch that nae butter pokes through (see fig. 5).

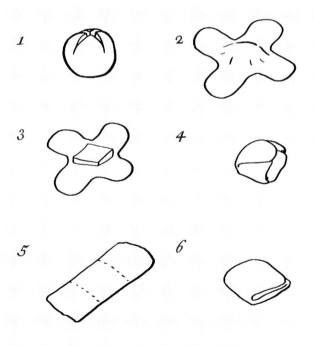

Brush off excess flour wi" a pastry brush. Fold in three (fold top end doon and the bottom end ower that, see fig. 6) and let it rest in the fridge for 20 minutes. Remove, gie it a quarter turn and then roll and fold as before.

I hope you're following this!

Repeat this another six times (seven foldings in all – nae mair), refrigerating for 20 minutes between each two rollings.

Let it rest in the fridge for several hours. When you come tae cut it you'll likely hae trimmings. Dinna scrunch them up into a ball or you'll lose the layers. If you want tae try tae save them, layer them up on top o' each ither. You'll use the scraps tae mak' the tops o' the vol-au-vents. They also make acceptable Palmiers (page 162).

Vol-au-vent cases
Roll the puff pastry to 1 cm thickness. Cut oot

roonds wi" whichever size o' cutter you prefer (mine is my 2-inch/5-cm scone cutter). Dip the cutter in water and cut oot roonds without twisting. Cover a baking sheet wi" baking parchment. Sprinkle wi" cold water. Turn the rounds upside doon onto the sheet. Mark the tops o' the patties wi" a cutter two sizes smaller, press it in a bit but dinna cut a' the way through. Put the dough in the fridge tae rest for 20 minutes.

Wi" the scraps o' pastry (remember, dinna scrunch the scraps, layer them) you're going tae mak' tops for the vol-au-vents. Roll this oot thinner than the bases and cut oot roonds wi" the smaller cutter. Place on the lined, watered baking sheet.

Preheat oven to 240°C, Gas 9. On putting the cases in the oven, turn that doon tae 230°C. Then efter 15 minutes turn that doon again tae 190°C.

Tak' oot o' the oven. Pick oot any o' the soggy

insides o' the cases and return tae the oven for a few minutes tae dry oot.

Filling method:

Melt the butter in a saucepan, add the flour and stir for a few minutes tae cook the flour. Tak' off the heat and add milk awfy gradually tae avoid lumps, beating strongly wi" a balloon whisk or a wooden spoon. Ensure there are no lumps at this stage (sieve it if you see any and then return tae the heat). Bring tae the boil stirring all the time until it thickens. Cover the cooked sauce wi" cling film so it disnae form a skin as it cools.

Fill the vol-au-vents wi" a mixture o' white sauce and your chosen savoury ingredient. Top wi" a pastry circle.

If you think your white sauce is a bit thick, beat a wee bitty single cream into it.

These are nice hot or cauld but we'll be

serving cauld for efternoon tea so season them well. Remember, cauld food needs mair seasoning than hot.

Whit a long recipe!

For sweet vol-au-vents fresh fruit can be bound together wi' whipped cream or pastry cream (page 126). Any awfy wet fruits such as pineapple should be squeezed o' excess juice first.

Ye got this ane right — Quiches Lorraine is the plural

Mini Quiches Lorraine

SHUT IT hORace

We ca'd these cheese flans in my day. You'll need wee tart tins for these or a 12-hole tart pan.

Shortcrust pastry

   200 g plain flour

   100 g butter (or a mixture of butter and
      lard)

   $\frac{1}{2}$ tsp salt

   Cold water (approx 75–100 ml)

Filling

   2 level tsps cornflour

   1 egg

   125 ml milk

   50–60 g cheese

   1 small onion, fried

   50 g cooked, smoked ham

Pastry

Preheat the oven to 200°C, 400°F, Gas 6. Grease and flour your tart pan.

Rub fat into the flour until it looks like breadcrumbs. Add the salt and then add, a wee bit at a time, the cold water. Mix it wi" a knife tae begin wi" (I have hot hands and dinna want tae melt the butter), then get in there wi" your hands and quickly mix tae a stiff consistency. Roll oot awfy thin, tae aboot 3 mm thickness.

Cut circles oot tae fit the tart pan holes. Bake blind for aboot 10 minutes (prick the pastry, put foil or baking paper in each case and fill wi" baking beans). Remove beans.

You could brush tart bottoms wi" beaten egg white and return tae the oven for a few minutes (tae seal and stop soggy bottoms later) if you wish. When done, remove from the oven and allow tae cool. At this point ensure none are stuck in the tart pan, but leave them there for the next stage.

Filling

Turn down the oven to 180°C, 350°F, Gas 4. Mix the cornflour and beaten egg. Add the milk, cheese, onion and ham. Season.

Pour into the pastry cases (dinna owerfill them) and top wi" a wee bitty mair grated cheese. Bake for around 10–15 minutes.

Tip — these are awfy cute and bite-sized when they're made in mini muffin tins. Dainty for efternoon tea, Like masel'!

Onion Tartlets

Makes 12 wee tarts or 24 wee totie tarts made in a mini muffin tray. Bonnie!

Shortcrust pastry

2 tbsps oil

1 tbsp butter

3 medium red onions, sliced

Good pinch of dried thyme

1 tsp balsamic vinegar

1 tsp sugar

Salt and white pepper

125 g soft cheese

Make shortcrust pastry (pages 81–83). Fry the onions in oil and butter till soft. Add thyme, vinegar and sugar and turn up heat tae caramelise. Season wi" salt and pepper. Fill each pastry case wi" the onions and top wi" a bit o' soft cheese. Bake at 200°C for around 10 minutes or till the cheese melts.

Mini Savoury Choux

Mrs Smythe insisted these were included. They're a big hit at her "at hames". (*They're ower la-di-da fir me.*)

Choux pastry

125 ml water

25 g butter

70 g plain flour

Pinch salt

2 small eggs

mini SaVouRY
shoes

Filling

Chicken liver pate

Whipping cream

Topping

2 tbsps quince jelly

1 tbsp water

Preheat the oven to 200°C, 400°F, Gas 6. Cover a

baking sheet wi" baking parchment. Bring the water and butter to the boil in a wee saucepan. Dinna boil for ower long. As soon as it reaches the boil add the flour and salt and beat thoroughly till smooth for around a minute. Spread on a plate to cool, covered in cling film. When cooler, though still a wee bitty warm, return to a clean bowl and beat in the two eggs gradually. Dinna mak' the dough ower runny. Stop adding egg when it gets tae a pipable consistency. Put into a piping bag.

Pipe into wee round blobs on the baking sheet. Leave plenty o' room between each one. Pat doon any pointy tops wi" a dampened finger (or they'll singe). Bake for aboot 15 minutes until risen and dry (tap them tae test). Mak' a wee hole in the bottom o' each tae let steam escape and return tae a medium oven tae dry oot a wee bit for a few mair minutes. Tak' oot o' the oven, allow tae cool.

Filling

Add a wee bitty whipping cream tae a shop-bought packet o' smooth chicken liver (or Brussels) pâté. Beat it tae a pipable consistency.

Attach a pointy-tipped nozzle tae a piping bag, fill the piping bag wi' pâté and fill the choux buns. Keep chilled till ready tae serve.

Topping

Heat the quince jelly and water in a saucepan till boiling. Brush or dribble a wee bit onto each choux bun tae glaze.

Savoury Pancakes

These are like genteel blinis ... no' yon deep fried crispy pancakes wi briedcrumbs on them.

200 g plain flour
1 level tsp salt
1 level tsp bicarbonate of soda
2 level tsp cream of tartar
1 egg
2 level tbsps chopped chives
250 ml milk
Salt and pepper

Sieve dry ingredients. Add egg and enough milk tae make a thick batter. Add chives.

Drop wee spoonfuls o' the mixture onto a fairly hot girdle or non-stick frying pan. Cook till the top surface starts tae bubble, turn and brown on the ither side. Cool in a clean tea towel. Particularly good wi" cream cheese and smoked salmon.
if you like that
88 kinda thing

Cheese Pastries

Mak' the pastry first - it needs tae rest in the fridge for an hour at least. An' keep it cauld while ye work wi" it - so it disnae get a soggy bottom when you bake it. Nothing worse!

Rough puff pastry
> 200 g plain flour
> 1 level tsp salt
> 150 g cold butter (or a mixture of
> 　　butter and lard)
> Juice of half a lemon
> 125 ml cold water

Filling
> 300 g crumbly cheese (like feta)
> 150-200 g fresh breadcrumbs
> 2 tbsps parsley, finely chopped
> 2 tbsps chives, finely chopped

1 red onion, finely chopped

¼ tsp black pepper

Salt and white pepper to taste

1 egg, beaten

Pastry

Cut the butter into fairly large pieces (chunks the size o' unshelled hazelnuts) and add tae the dry ingredients. Dinna rub the butter in wi" the fingers, leave it as it is.

Add lemon juice to the bowl. Then, a wee bitty at a time, add water and mix to an elastic consistency wi" the fingers. Turn it oot o' the bowl and work lightly till it just comes together. Rest the pastry for 30 minutes in the fridge.

Roll into a rectangle. Brush off excess flour, fold in three (like a business letter – no' that I send ony o' those!), seal the edges by pressing wi" the rolling pin, gie it a quarter turn. Roll oot again.

Repeat rolling, folding and turning another two or three times or till butter is evenly distributed. Rest for at least 30 minutes in the fridge before using.

Filling the pastry

Preheat the oven to 200°C, 400°F, Gas 6. Grate the cheese and mix the filling ingredients (all except the egg) together. (Dinna ower-salt as some cheeses can already be salty.) Roll oot the pastry into a long rectangle. Place the filling along the pastry in a line. Trim the pastry all along one side o' the filling, then on the other leaving enough room to roll and seal it.

Brush the length o' the pastry wi'' beaten egg or water and then roll it up and seal it. Cut shallow slashes in the top o' the roll and then cut the roll up into wee cheese rolls.

Place on a greased baking sheet and bake for aboot 20 minutes or until the pastry is puffed and golden and the cheese melted inside.

Oatcakes

A guid Scottish spread needs oatcakes. These were requested tae be in this book by Maw Smith's Grandad Jack when we were puttin' this together – they're his favourites. Oor ain Granpaw Broon loves them tae. Richt enough, I've never kent him tae turn doon ony food. Wee totie oatcakes wi" savoury toppings are richt genteel lookin'. I've seen smoked salmon and cream cheese on oatcakes – wi" sweet pickled cucumber tae. I never ate it though.

225 g oatmeal

40 g lard or dripping

$\frac{1}{2}$ tsp salt

Boiling water

Add salt to oatmeal. Melt dripping and add a wee bitty boilin' water. Mix the liquid wi" dry ingredients to a soft paste. Add more boilin' water *if required. Roll as thinly as possible into a circle and cut into quarters. Rub wi" dry oatmeal tae whiten.*

Cook on a fairly hot girdle. When cooked on one side, dry off in a cool oven or under the grill.

N⁰ 23

MACDUFF'S
SCOTTISH FOODS OF QUALITY

Ingredients: 1 kg redcurrants
Sugar
750 ml water
Method:
Wash fruit without removing stalks. Put in preserving pan with water and simmer till quite tender. Mash well. Strain through scalded jelly bag and allow to drip overnight. Measure the juice and allow 1 kg sugar to each 1250 mls. Heat juice and dissolve sugar in it. Boil rapidly to setting point. Skim, cool and stir before potting in sterilised jars. Cover with circles of greaseproof paper and jar lids while still warm.

Redcurrant Jelly

N⁰ 20

MACDUFF'S
SCOTTISH FOODS OF QUALITY

Ingredients:
1 kg damsons
Sugar (1 kg sugar for each 1250 mls juice)
500 g cooking apples
Water
Method:
Wash fruit and chop up apples. Put all in a jelly pan and cover with water. Simmer slowly till tender. Mash well and strain overnight through a jelly bag or muslin. Measure juice and allow 1 kg sugar for each 1250 mls juice. Dissolve sugar in juice, then boil rapidly until setting point is reached. Skim, quickly pour into sterilised jars and cover.

Damson Jelly

The Secret Of Good Pastry

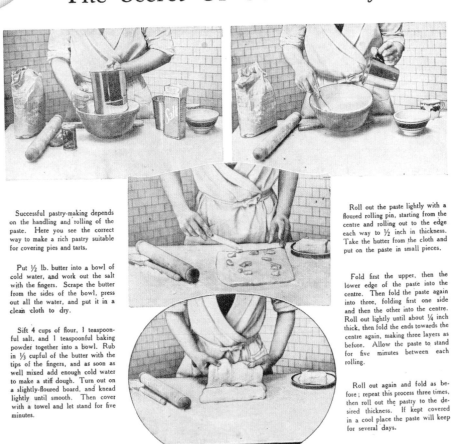

Successful pastry-making depends on the handling and rolling of the paste. Here you see the correct way to make a rich pastry suitable for covering pies and tarts.

Put ½ lb. butter into a bowl of cold water, and work out the salt with the fingers. Scrape the butter from the sides of the bowl, press out all the water, and put it in a clean cloth to dry.

Sift 4 cups of flour, 1 teaspoonful salt, and 1 teaspoonful baking powder together into a bowl. Rub in ⅓ cupful of the butter with the tips of the fingers, and as soon as well mixed add enough cold water to make a stiff dough. Turn out on a slightly-floured board, and knead lightly until smooth. Then cover with a towel and let stand for five minutes.

Roll out the paste lightly with a floured rolling pin, starting from the centre and rolling out to the edge each way to ½ inch in thickness. Take the butter from the cloth and put on the paste in small pieces.

Fold first the upper, then the lower edge of the paste into the centre. Then fold the paste again into three, folding first one side and then the other into the centre. Roll out lightly until about ¼ inch thick, then fold the ends towards the centre again, making three layers as before. Allow the paste to stand for five minutes between each rolling.

Roll out again and fold as before; repeat this process three times, then roll out the pastry to the desired thickness. If kept covered in a cool place the paste will keep for several days.

When making pastry have all the utensils required as clean and cold as possible, and work in a very cool place. The colder the pastry is kept during the making the lighter it will be. Always sprinkle flour over the board and pastry through a flour sifter, as this makes the pastry lighter and finer.

Cakes and
Sweet Pastries

Why do the twins eat so fast?

We want to eat as much as possible before we lose our appetites

Victoria Sandwich

Yer basic Victoria Sandwich recipe can be used tae
mak' dozens o' different cakes: add a bit o' cocoa
here – add a bit o' zest there. It can also be used
tae mak' wee fairy cakes too, or cupcakes as they
like tae ca' them noo. It's easy tae mind tae: same
weights o' a' the basic ingredients (but no' the extras
mind – 175 g lemon zest wid be quite nippy!).

175 g caster sugar

175 g soft butter

175 g self-raising flour or 175 g plain
   flour and $1\frac{1}{2}$ tsps baking powder

3 eggs/175 g eggs, at room temperature,
   beaten (or alternatively, weigh three
   eggs and use same weight of S R
   flour, butter and sugar: less waste!)

Cream the sugar and butter together till fluffy, add beaten eggs slowly, and a wee drap at a time, and beat well. Add flour and eggs alternately (tae avoid curdling, which deflates all your hard work beating the butter and sugar together).

Put in two greased and floured 18-cm/7-inch sandwich tins. Bake at 160°C for 20–25 minutes until the sponge springs back tae the touch. A skewer should come oot clean.

Turn oot onto a wire rack tae cool. When cold, sandwich together wi" jam and dredge wi" icing sugar. (Awfy slimming!)

All-in-one method
(Ye might get a slightly heavier, smaller sponge, wi" a bigger crumb than the above method but it'll still be guid.) Put a' the ingredients (all at room temperature) intae a bowl and beat till well mixed, for 1–2 minutes. Bake and decorate as above.

Alternatives

They dinna dae this at my SWRI group – they're sticklers for tradition – but Victoria sandwich is braw wi" rasp jam an' fresh whipped cream (whit isnae?).

Or sandwich it together wi" butter icing (page 137) and cover wi" water icing (page 136) o' a thick pouring consistency. The water icing should run doon the sides an' a hot dry knife can be used tae spread it a' ower.

Cupcakes

A few years ago a'body suddenly started calling wee sponges cupcakes. We aye called them fairy cakes. And they suddenly started getting ower-big and covered in ower-much American-style buttercream (pages 137-8). I often think there's mair icing than cake. Maybe that's what you like though. Ah wid suggest that flavoured water icing is a bit mair genteel.

Fairy cakes

Prepare a 12-hole muffin tin wi" paper cases. Follow the ingredients and the method for Victoria Sandwich. Half-fill the paper cake cases and bake for aboot 15-20 minutes or until a skewer comes oot cleanly or the tops are springy tae the touch. Decorate wi" water icing (page 136), butter icing (page 137), or ganache (page 139-141).

Butterfly cakes

You used tae see these a lot at bairns' birthday parties. Maybe they're a bit childish for efternoon tea. I'm a big bairn though.

Mak' fairy cakes as I've described a'ready. When cold, cut a slice frae the top o' each cake and cut in twa across the middle. Beat some double cream wi" 1 tsp caster sugar and a few drops o' vanilla extract. Pipe cream on each cake, place cut tops on cream tae form wings and dust wi" icing sugar.

Favourite Recipes

6

2 egg yolks
3 egg whites
⅓ cup/1½ oz/45 g icing
  sugar
⅓ cup/1½ oz/45 g flour

¼ tsp vanilla
⅛ tsp salt
Raspberry jam
Whipped cream

Beat the egg whites till stiff. Beat in sugar gradually. Beat and add the yolks and the vanilla. Sift and fold in the flour and salt. Put into a piping bag and pipe into fingers on a baking sheet covered with baking parchment, sprinkle with icing sugar. Bake for 8 minutes at 180°C. Remove carefully. Put together in pairs with whipped cream and jam. Decorate with water icing.

Ladyship Sponges

Chocolate Cake

Ella Brownlee says the "naked cake" is a' the rage the noo. Bit lazy if you ask me. Sprinkle the top wi" a few chopped nuts or some coconut afore you bake it tae take the bare look aff it at least. Bake either as several wee cakes or as an 18-cm/7-inch sandwich cake.

175 g caster sugar

175 g soft butter

150 g self-raising flour or 150 g plain
flour and 1 ½ tsps baking powder

25 g cocoa powder

1 tsp of chicory essence

3 eggs (175 g eggs)

Preheat the oven to 160°C, 325°F, Gas 3. Grease and flour two 18-cm/7-inch sandwich tins.

Cream the sugar and butter together till fluffy. Add beaten eggs a wee bit at a time, and beat well. Add flour, cocoa powder and chicory essence, and beat until smooth. (Add flour and eggs in alternate spoonfuls if you wish.) As soon as all flour is mixed in smoothly pour into sandwich tins. Bake at 160°C for aboot 20–25 minutes. When cold, sandwich together wi" jam, whipped cream, or buttercream (page 138) and dredge wi" icing sugar.

Battenberg Cake

Ingredients as per Victoria Sandwich

    (page 97)

Red food colouring

Buttercream (page 138)

Jam

Marzipan (page 143)

Grease a 16-24 cm square tin. Line with baking parchment, but fold a V doon the centre o' the *parchment so that you can effectively divide your tin into two. (This can be more easily done using foil-backed baking parchment.)*

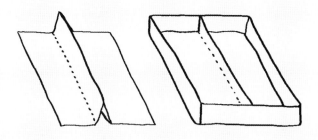

Put half o' the mixture in one side o' the tin, colour the ither half pink and put into the ither side o' the tin.

Bake at 190°C (375°F, Gas 5) for aboot 20 minutes or until cooked. Allow to cool in the tin.

When cold, cut each half in two by length and sandwich together alternately wi' buttercream (or jam if you prefer). Press well together (no' too hard, mind).

Roll oot the marzipan thinly into an oblong big enough to cover the whole cake.

Spread the ootside o' the cake wi" buttercream or jam, and lay it along one edge o' the marzipan and fold it carefully ower. Tidy the ends wi" a sharp knife.

Queen Victoria (of Victoria Sponge fame) was awfy fond o' German cakes. When her granddaughter, Princess Victoria o' Hesse-Darmstadt wis gettin' married tae Prince Louis o' Battenberg, the Royal Chefs (of Royal Icing fame) came up wi' Battenberg Cake. The sponge wis twa different colours and put together like the check on a polisman's hat. A bit later, there was a World War and Louis wanted tae be on oor side so they changed their German name to Mountbatten. So that's why the cake should be called Mountbatten Cake. Some fowk say this isnae who invented it cos there was Domino Cake and Neapolitan Roll, but surely Domino cake would hae spots, and a roll wid be roond, no square!

Fatless Sponge

This is a braw sponge – nae need tae dae onything ower fancy wi" it. Cream an' fruit is fine wi" this – nae rich icing needed. A'thing in moderation I say, but if you're watching your cholesterol this is the cake tae try (just wi" jam).

4 eggs
150 g caster sugar
100 g plain flour

Preheat the oven to 180°C, 350°F, Gas 4. Grease two 18-cm/7-inch sandwich tins and dust wi" a mixture o' flour and sugar, or cut oot and line the base wi" a circle o' greaseproof paper.

Using an electric mixer, beat the sugar and eggs to a thick cream (should be white in colour).

Fold in flour awfy gently, it's no' cement you're mixing. Pour into tin.

Bake at 180°C for 25–30 minutes or until it springs back tae the touch and starts tae leave the sides o' the tin. When cool, sandwich wi" whipped cream and fresh fruit. Dredge wi" icing sugar.

Favourite Recipes

19

1 kg hulled strawberries
1 kg sugar

Heat strawberries in a jelly pan until juice flows (about 15 minutes). Add sugar and boil quickly for 15 minutes. Skim, cool and stir before potting in sterilised jars.

Cover with circles of greaseproof paper and jar lids while still warm.

Note: Must be made from dry, firm fruit. It does not gel, but is syrupy.

Strawberry Jam

Favourite Recipes

7

Shortcrust pastry
Egg white
½ cup/4 oz/120 g sugar
½ cup/about 4 oz/120 g strawberries, chopped

2 cups/1 pint water
2 tsps arrowroot
Strawberries
Cream, whipped

Line little tart tins with shortcrust pastry and bake blind at 180°C for 10 minutes. Brush pastry with egg white. Return to the oven for two minutes. Bring the sugar, strawberries and water to the boil to release the juices from

the strawberries. Blend arrowroot with two teaspoons water in a bowl. Strain the juice. Add the juice to the arrowroot, mixing thoroughly. Fill with cream. Place strawberries on cream and pour syrup over while still warm.

Strawberry Tarts

Swiss Roll

This is the Bairn's favourite. She likes tae help me roll it up – though it can get a bitty squashed if she's been ower enthusiastic.

Use the Fatless Sponge recipe (page 107) but preheat the oven to 220°C, 420°F or Gas 7.

Grease and paper a large flat rectangular tin. Make as described in Fatless Sponge recipe. Pour into the greased and papered tin and bake for aboot 10 minutes or until the sponge springs back tae the touch.

Sift caster sugar onto some greaseproof paper a wee bitty bigger than the sponge, on top o' a large clean tea towel. Turn oot onto the paper, trim the crisp long edges, spread wi" hot jam and roll up firmly (using the paper and tea towel tae help).

To serve, dust wi" more caster sugar.

Chocolate Swiss roll

Replace 25 g o' flour wi" 25 g o' cocoa or drinking chocolate – depends on yer ain taste. My preference is drinking chocolate – it's mair delicate and suits the sponge better.

To fill wi" cream – roll up wi" a piece o' greaseproof paper inside and when cool unroll gently and fill wi" a cream filling.

Meringues

Agnes is a dab hand wi" meringues – she aye says that wi" meringues you're drying oot slowly – ye're no' bakin'. So you cannae be in ony hurry when ye're makin' them. The proportion o' sugar is 50 g for each egg white (and maist eggs contain aboot 25 g o' egg white). So, for three whites you need 150 g caster sugar.

3 egg whites

150 g caster sugar

Preheat the oven to 60°C. Whip wi" an electric beater in an awfy clean metal or glass bowl. Any fat (and that includes egg yolk) will ruin yer meringue.

Whip the egg whites till they reach soft peaks and then add the sugar. Whip till glossy wi" firm peaks. Spoon onto a baking sheet in the size and shape you prefer. (Meringues winna grow that much as they cook.) Bake at 60-70°C for aboot six hours (or overnight if you're no' worried aboot leaving the oven on).

Take oot o' the oven and keep in an air-tight container.

Sandwich together wi" whipped cream. Meringue goes well wi" sharp fruits.

Brandy Snaps

So does paw if you hide his falsers

Ye need tae work quickly wi" these and watch oot for burny fingers! They will spread oot a lot efter they've been in the oven so leave plenty o' room between spoonfuls. Horace says brandy snaps were made on market days in medieval times in France and Belgium, and now they're eaten a' ower the world. If you shape these ower a greased, upside-doon cup you can make them into brandy baskets. (Granpaw says can he just hae the brandy? – ye can keep yer basket.)

50 g butter

50 g brown sugar

2 tbsps golden syrup

1 tsp ground ginger

50 g plain flour

Preheat the oven to 180°C (350°F, Gas 4).

Melt the butter. Add the sugar and syrup and heat till it has dissolved, dinna stir, and dinna let it boil. Take aff the heat and stir in the flour and spice. Drop in teaspoonfuls onto a baking sheet covered in baking parchment, space them around 15 cm/6 inches apart.

Bake at 180°C for aboot 7–10 minutes or until they bubble and look lacy. Take oot o' the oven. While still warm, roll each one roond the greased handle o' a wooden spoon. Slip aff when cool enough.

Just afore serving, fill wi' Chantilly Cream

Nº 26

MACDUFF'S

SCOTTISH FOODS OF QUALITY

Ingredients: 300 ml whipping cream
1 vanilla pod
Icing sugar, to taste

Method:
Put the cream in a bowl. Cut a vanilla pod in half lengthways with a sharp knife and scrape out the seeds. Add the seeds to the creams. (Keep the pod and use another time.)'

Whip the cream until it forms soft peaks. Add icing sugar, to taste, and mix in gently.

Chantilly Cream

Another recipe o' Mrs Smythe's.
How dae ye even say that?

Millefeuille

it's pronounced
"meel—foy"

Ah'd ca' this a Vanilla Slice but whit dae Ah ken?

350 g puff pastry (pages 72-76)

Icing sugar (for dusting)

300 ml whipping cream or double cream,

    or pastry cream (page 126) and

    whipping cream mixed together

Raspberries or ither fresh fruit

Preheat the oven to 200°C, 400°F, Gas. Roll oot your puff pastry thinly (aboot 3-5 mm). Line a large baking sheet wi" parchment and dust wi" icing sugar. Put the pastry on the sheet and dust that wi" icing sugar as well. Put anither sheet o' parchment on top and then put a heavy baking sheet on top o' this (to keep the puff pastry from rising a' uneven). Weigh it doon wi" something if your baking sheets are quite light. Bake for 25–30 minutes till the pastry is a guid broon colour. Allow to cool.

Each millefeuille will hae three rectangles o' pastry in it. Even-up the edges o' the pastry. Then cut into three pieces o' the same size. Use a ruler – I'm no' kiddin'! They're going tae look awfy messy if they're a' different sizes. Once ye've cut one you can use that as a guide for the next. The trick to cutting this pastry is tae use an awfy sharp, long knife and to work wi" quick, confident chops. Divide these long strips further intae rectangles o' equal size. Layer-up your pastry rectangles wi" a filling o' cream or pastry cream and fruit.

Dust liberally wi" icing sugar.

Apple Turnovers

Flaky pastry

    200 g plain flour

    100 ml cold water (approx)

    150 g butter, or a mixture of butter and
        lard, softened

    Pinch salt

    Juice of half a lemon

Filling

    4 Bramley apples – peeled, cored and sliced

    2 tbsps butter

    200 g brown sugar

    1 tsp cinnamon

    1 tbsp cornflour

    1 tbsp water

Pastry:

Divide the fat into four equal portions. Add salt to flour and rub in one quarter o' the fat. Add lemon juice to the flour and mix in. A wee bit at a time, add water and mix tae an elastic consistency. Turn oot onto a floured work-surface. Work lightly wi" the heel o' your hand. Wrap the dough in cling film and rest in the fridge for 20 minutes. Meanwhile, hae a wee rest yersel'!

Roll intae an oblong and place one quarter o' the butter in wee pieces dotted on two thirds o' the dough (see fig. 1 on next page). Fold up one third *(see fig. 2) and down one third (see fig. 3, dough and fat should lie in alternate layers). Seal the edges, gie it a quarter turn, and roll oot again.*

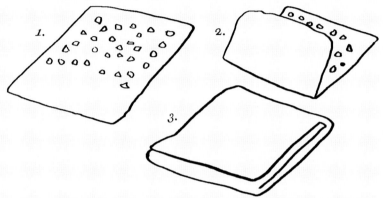

Repeat wi" more butter. Rest the pastry in the fridge for 20 minutes, then repeat the rollings twice more (that's five rollings). Leave tae rest for 30 minutes in the fridge. Time for a wee cuppa.

Cooking and filling

Preheat the oven to 200°C, 400°F, Gas 6. Melt the butter in a large pan over medium heat. Add the peeled, sliced apples. Cook for a few minutes, then add the broon sugar and cinnamon, and cook for a few more minutes. Mix the cornflour with 1 tablespoon water. Pour over the apples and mix well. Cook until sauce has thickened then take it aff the heat an' let it cool a bit.

Roll oot the pastry to aboot 5 mm thickness and trim to make a rectangle. Cut into wee squares. Spoon apple mixture onto the centre o' each square. Fold over frae corner tae corner. Make a wee hole on the top to let the steam escape. Place the turnovers on a baking sheet, leaving aboot 1 inch between them. Brush wi" milk or egg.

Bake for aboot 25 minutes until the turnovers are golden broon. Cool completely before icing.

Other fruit pastries

Place two fruit halves e.g. plums, pears, peaches etc, on each pastry square and sprinkle wi" sugar or honey. Bake 15–20 minutes at 180°C or until golden broon (of course).

Tarts

For all the tarts: Preheat the oven to 190°C, 350°F, Gas 5, and grease and flour a 12-hole tart pan or individual tart cases. After making the pastry, let it rest in the fridge. Roll oot the pastry thinly, cut oot 12 roonds to fit the holes in the tart pans. Put a piece o' foil on each base, fill wi" baking beans and bake blind for 10-15 minutes.

Sweet rich shortcrust pastry

I like tae replace water in short pastry wi" 1 whole egg tae 200 g flour.

> 250 g plain flour
>
> Pinch salt
>
> 125 g unsalted butter, chilled
>
> 25 g caster sugar
>
> 1 egg (or about 75–100 ml water)

Mix the flour and salt together. Cut the cold butter in wee cubes and rub into flour. Add the sugar and mix through. Beat the egg and add. Mix wi" a knife till the dough comes together. Add water if ye need it. Tip oot onto a floured work-surface, and knead until you hae a smooth, dough. Wrap in cling film and rest for at least an hour in the fridge.

Tip: Tae avoid soggy-bottomed tarts brush the just-cooked pastry (after baking blind) wi" beaten egg white, and return to the oven for a few mair minutes.

Biscuit pastry

200 g plain flour

125 g butter

40 g caster sugar

Pinch salt

1 egg, beaten

Cream butter and sugar, work in the flour and salt and enough egg tae form a stiff paste. Rest in the fridge then use as required. This makes braw tarts but it can be hard to work wi" if you're trying to roll it thin – keep it cold and this will help.

Pastry for keeping (Nett's recipe)

450 g plain flour

285 g butter

115 g caster sugar

$\frac{1}{2}$ *egg (beaten)*

Pinch salt

Pinch baking soda

I make this at Christmas and use for my mince pies

Cream the butter and sugar together, and mix in the egg. Add salt and baking soda to the flour. Gradually work the flour into the butter and sugar mixture. Rest (the dough, I mean) then use as required. Dinna roll it oot all at once – cut it into quarters. Roll up in cling film and it will keep in the fridge for 3 weeks.

Lemon curd filling

This is Maw Smith's microwave version. If, like me, you dinna hae a microwave you can still easily mak' it in a pan.

200 g caster sugar

3 eggs

Juice of 4 lemons

Zest of 3 lemons

100 g unsalted
    butter

Nº 18

MACDUFF'S

SCOTTISH FOODS OF QUALITY

Ingredients:
50 g butter
2 lemons (juice and grated zest)
150 g sugar
4 egg yolks

Method:
Grate the zest from the lemons (take care not to include bitter pith). Melt butter and pour into a bowl with the sugar and grated lemon rind. Juice the two lemons and whisk up the egg yolks. Add to the bowl. Put the bowl in a pan of hot water (not touching the water), stir over the heat till the mixture thickens. Put into a jar and store in the fridge.

Lemon Curd

In a glass bowl, whisk together the sugar and eggs until smooth. Stir in the lemon juice, lemon zest and butter. Cook in the microwave, stopping at 1 minute intervals, to stir, until the mixture is thick enough to coat the back o' a metal spoon.

Pour into wee sterilised jars. (To sterilise jars wash in hot, soapy water, rinse in hot water, dry wi" a clean tea towel and place in the oven for aboot 20 minutes at 100°C.) Store for up to three weeks in the fridge.

Lemon or lime filling

1 tin (397 g) condensed milk

2 egg yolks

Juice of 2 lemons or 3 limes

2 egg whites

2 level tbsps caster sugar

Beat together the condensed milk, egg yolks and lemon or lime juice. Pour into cooked pastry cases.

Beat the egg whites and gradually add the caster sugar. Continue beating till egg white is stiff wi" peaks. Pipe onto the tarts and bake at 190°C, 350°F, Gas 5, for about 15 minutes or until golden broon.

Pastry cream

250 ml milk

Vanilla extract or a vanilla pod

2 egg yolks

25 g cornflour

30–40 g sugar

If you're using it, split the vanilla pod and take oot the seeds. In a saucepan, heat the milk wi" vanilla seeds and pod and simmer. In a glass bowl, whisk yolks, sugar, vanilla extract (if using) and cornflour together till pale. Add the milk to the eggs, and whisk. Strain the mixure and return to the pan. Slowly bring to the boil, whisking a' the time. When thick, pour into a clean bowl and cover surface wi" cling film and leave to cool.

Fruit glaze or sauce

125 ml fruit juice

1 level tsp arrowroot

Squeeze lemon juice

1 tsp sugar

Blend arrowroot wi" some fruit juice. Pour into saucepan wi the rest o' the fruit juice, lemon juice and sugar. Boil for only 1 minute (arrowroot mixtures get runny if overheated).

Caramel filling

Now, you could boil a tin o' condensed milk for hours tae mak' this. However, I think it's actually cheaper tae just buy a tin o' caramel oot the supermarket (in the same aisle as the condensed milk). Ye'll save on your gas bill and it's exactly the same stuff. (And I'm aye feart the tin will explode.) It's sometimes ca'd "dulce de leche". Fill pastry cases wi" caramel and sprinkle the tops wi" grated dark chocolate. Easy!

Fruit tarts

In autumn when I'm at the But an' Ben, there are plenty o' aipples and pears for making intae tarts. Bake tart cases blind, then fill wi" sliced fruit, glaze and bake for aboot anither 15 minutes.

In summer there are braw strawberries an' raspberries. Spoon or pipe pastry cream into the base o' the cases and then top wi" fresh fruit and a glaze (page 127). Autumn fruits like plums can be stoned and skinned and served fresh tae. When a' the fruit is done ... (see pic above) tinned peaches it is!

Tarts are always Popular

Custard Tarts are equally nice served hot for lunch or cold for tea.

Tarts with fruit and creamy fillings can never be made too often. Recipes for pastries used will be found on page 23.

Lemon Tarts.

Short crust.   4 oz. butter.
4 oz. castor sugar.   2 eggs.
     1 lemon.

Cream the butter and sugar well together. Beat each egg in separately, then add the juice of the lemon and the rind, finely grated. Let the mixture stand in a cool, dry place for 24 hours. Then bake in patty tins lined with short crust for 20 minutes. This makes 18 tarts.

Raisin Nut Tart.

Grated rind and juice of 2 lemons.   2 cupfuls seeded raisins.
Grated rind and juice of 1 orange.   1¼ cupfuls sugar.
1 cupful chopped walnuts.   1 cupful brown sugar.
     Short crust.
3 tablespoonfuls cornflour.

Short crust filled with a delicious fruity filling makes Raisin Nut Tart an enjoyable affair. Arrange the pastry in strips on the top and ice with vanilla icing when the tart is cold.

Line a deep sandwich tin with the pastry. Cook together all the ingredients except the cornflour. When the mixture boils, thicken it with the cornflour mixed with 1 tablespoonful of cold water. Put the mixture into the lined tin and cover with a lid of pastry strips. Brush over with cold water. Bake for 40 minutes. When cold ice with a little Vanilla Icing (recipe on page 17).

Banana Pie.

Short crust.   2 bananas.
2 tablespoonfuls sugar.   2 egg whites.
A pinch of salt.   Essence of almonds.
Lemon juice.   Whipped cream.

Roll out the pastry thinly and line a greased sandwich tin with it. Decorate the edge with an extra strip of pastry, fluting it neatly, prick the bottom and bake in a hot oven for 12 minutes. Rub the bananas through a sieve and add to them the sugar, salt and unbeaten egg whites. Beat all together till stiff and frothy, then flavour with almond essence and a squeeze of lemon juice. Fill the pastry case with the mixture and bake in a moderate oven for 20 minutes. When cool decorate the top with the stiffly-whipped cream.

Blackberry Tartlets.

Short crust.   2 oz. blackberry jelly.
2 oz. butter.   2 oz. cake crumbs.
12 drops orange-   1 oz. sugar.
flower water.   1 dessertspoonful
1 egg.   chopped Brazil nuts.
     1 oz. ground rice.

Cream the butter with the sugar. Beat in the egg yolk, the crumbs, rice, nuts and orange-flower water. Add the white of egg, whipped to a froth. Line patty tins with the pastry and put a teaspoonful of blackberry jelly in each. Nearly fill with the mixture, sprinkle a little chopped nuts on top of each and bake in a moderate oven for ½ hour.

Chocolate Tarts.

3 macaroon biscuits.   2 tablespoonfuls
½ pint milk.   grated chocolate.
2 egg yolks.   Castor sugar.
Vanilla.   Short crust.

Line a dozen patty tins with short crust. Melt the chocolate in a small quantity of the milk, then add the rest of the milk with the biscuit crumbs and let them simmer for 10 minutes. Remove from the fire and add sugar to taste, flavouring, and the egg yolks. Mix well and fill the lined tins with the mixture. Lay some narrow strips of pastry over the top of each, and bake in a good oven for 20 minutes.

Custard Tarts.

½ pint milk.   2 eggs.
1 dessertspoonful   Cake crumbs.
sugar.   Vanilla.
     Short crust.

Line a dozen patty tins with the short crust, which has been rolled out thinly, and bake them until the pastry is set, but not brown. Meanwhile prepare the custard. Put the milk into a saucepan to heat. Beat up the eggs with the sugar and flavouring to taste, and pour the hot milk on to them, stirring all the time. Then strain, and fill the pastry shells with the custard and return them to the oven till the custard is set and nicely browned.

Ginger Tartlets.

Short crust.   1 egg.
2 oz. butter.   2 oz. sugar.
1 oz. flour.   1 oz. rice flour.
½ teaspoonful baking   1 dessertspoonful
powder.   ginger syrup.
2 oz. preserved ginger.

Line patty tins with the rolled-out short crust.

Cream the butter, add the egg yolk, sugar, ginger syrup and flours, sieved. Mix well, then stir in the chopped ginger, the baking powder and the frothed egg white. Half-fill the pastry cases with the mixture, and bake for 20 minutes in a good oven. Dredge with sugar and remove from the tins.

Lemon Meringue Tart.

Short crust.   2 cupfuls water.
4 tablespoonfuls corn-   2 tablespoonfuls flour.
flour.   1½ cupfuls sugar.
2 eggs.   4 tablespoonfuls lemon
2 teaspoonfuls grated   juice.
lemon rind.   1 teaspoonful salt.
     1 teaspoonful baking powder.

Line a pie-plate with the paste, prick the bottom, trim the edges and bake in a hot oven for 10 minutes. Now make the filling. Put the water on to boil. Mix the cornflour, flour, 1 cupful of sugar with ½ cupful cold water until smooth. Mix in the egg yolks, slightly beaten, and add slowly to the boiling water. Cook 5 minutes, stirring constantly, then remove from the fire and add the lemon juice, rind and salt. Pour into the baked crust and cover with meringue made by frothing stiffly the egg whites with ½ cupful sugar and the baking powder. Bake in a moderate oven for 10 minutes.

Spiced American Tart.

½ lb. apples.   ½ lb. sultanas.
1 lemon rind.   2½ gills cold water.
2 teaspoonfuls corn-   Mixed spice.
flour.   2 dessertspoonfuls
1 oz. almonds.   granulated sugar.
     Short crust.

Wash the sultanas and soak them in 2 gills of the water for ½ hour. Then turn them into a saucepan, add the sugar and a good pinch of mixed spice and stew gently for 2 minutes. Draw the pan aside from the flame. Mix the cornflour to a smooth paste with ½ gill of water. Stir the syrup from the sultanas on to it. Turn into a pan and boil for a few minutes. Draw the pan aside, add the sultanas, grated lemon rind, chopped almonds, and peeled, grated apples. Mix all together and leave till cold. Roll out the pastry and line a sandwich tin with it. Put in the mixture, cover with a lid of pastry and bake for 20 minutes in a hot oven. When cool decorate with a little Vanilla Icing (recipe on page 17) coloured with carmine.

Strawberry Tart.

Short crust.   Strawberries.
2 tablespoonfuls sugar.   1 tablespoonful water.

Syrup:

½ cupful sugar.   ½ cupful strawberries.
2 cupfuls boiling water.   1 tablespoonful corn-
     flour.

Line a pie-plate with the short crust and bake in a hot oven for 15 minutes. After baking, brush the edges with hot syrup made by combining the sugar and boiling water, and return to the oven for 2 minutes until the syrup hardens. Fill the baked crust with fresh strawberries and cover with the syrup. Bring to the boil the sugar, strawberries and boiling water, and strain. Add the cornflour, which has been blended with a little cold water, and cook over a hot fire for 2 minutes, stirring all the time. Remove from the fire and beat hard, then return to a low heat and cook gently till thick. Pour while hot over the strawberries and set aside to cool. Before serving top with whipped cream.

Topped with delicately browned meringue, Lemon Meringue Tart is a dainty dish for tea. Serve it cut in generous wedges. It is also delicious as a pudding, and can be used either hot or cold with a nice sweet sauce.

Bride's Slices

In the past there was nae big fancy three-tiered cake at a wedding feast – these bride's, or bridal, slices would hae been the celebration cakes. They're quite rich and fruity like wedding cake.

Sweet shortcrust pastry (page 122)

50 g butter

100 g caster sugar

100 g cherries

2 eggs

200 g currants or sultanas or mixture of both

1 tsp mixed spice

½ tsp vanilla essence

6 tbsps crushed digestive biscuits

Jam

Marzipan (page 143)

Preheat the oven to 180°C, 350, Gas 4. Line a Swiss roll tin wi" sweet shortcrust pastry (page 122). Chill. Cream butter and sugar, add eggs, beat. Add biscuits, mixed spice and vanilla. Add fruit and mix well. Spread ower the pastry.

Bake for 45 minutes to 1 hour. When cool, spread wi" an awfy thin layer o' jam. Cover wi" a thin layer o' marzipan. If you wish, top wi" royal icing too (page 141) or dust wi" icing sugar. Cut into fingers. Instead o' fruit, try using the equivalent weight o' mincemeat wi" the crushed biscuits.

When you are stressed you eat ice cream cakes and sweets ... because stressed is desserts spelled backwards

Chocolate Eclairs

Choux pastry (page 35)

Pastry cream (page 126)

Whipping cream

Follow the method for choux pastry on page 35, except pipe the pastry into a finger shape. Make pastry cream (page 126). Allow to cool. Whip 100 ml o' whipping cream into the pastry cream. Cool the pastries, split and fill wi" pastry cream. Ice wi" chocolate ganache (page 139) or water icing (page 136).

eh cLaReS aRe OOR faVOURiTes bY Ae TWin

Making a Celebration Cake

Getting a group o' bakers in a room and trying tae get them a' tae agree on whit's the best method tae make such-and-such is a bit like a debate in parliament – except the MPs sometimes agree. Annie uses Victoria Sponge – so does Jessie. I'd say for a big, layered cake, choose a guid moist Madeira rather than a Victoria Sandwich. The weight o' the coverings and fillings can crack a light, dry sponge. Madeira also keeps a bit longer. A guid Madeira will keep for a week. Madeira cake neednae be stodgy if you follow these instructions:

* All ingredients should be at room temperature.

* Dinna add cold eggs tae warm butter – the mixture will curdle.

* Use a guid-tasting butter. Pick the dear stuff.

* Beat the butter and sugar till awfy fluffy.

* Substitute a little oil for some o' the butter and the cake will be moister – no' too much though.

* Add a wee teaspoon o' glycerine as well.

Madeira cake

175 g softened butter

175 g caster sugar

225 g self-raising flour

3 large eggs

Granpaw walks into a cake shop. "How much is that wee cake?" he asks. The baker says, "All my cakes are £1." Whit a bargain, thinks Granpaw. "I'll have that one then," he says, pointing to the biggest cake wi' the maist cream. The baker says "£5 please." "Whit?" says Granpaw, "I thocht a' yer cakes were a poun'?" "That's madeira cake!" Boom, boom.

Pre-heat the oven to 160°C, 325°F, Gas 3. Grease and line an 18-cm/7-inch round cake tin. Wrap the outside o' the tin wi" corrugated cardboard and tie wi" string.

Beat the butter and sugar together till fluffy. Beat in the eggs a little at a time. If it looks like it's curdling add a spoonful o' flour and beat thoroughly till the mixture is smooth again. Fold in the rest o' the flour. Add a flavouring such as lemon zest, vanilla, coffee (espresso), desiccated coconut. Mix thoroughly. Spoon into the cake tin.

Bake for aboot 60 minutes in the middle o' the oven. If the sponge is springy and a skewer comes oot clean it's ready. If it leaves an indentation, cook the cake longer. Ovens can be awfy unpredictable. Just like fowk! Leave in the tin till it's cool afore carefully turning oot onto a wire rack. Dinna go thumping the cake aroond once it's oot the oven and still hot or ye'll flatten it! Ca' canny!

Water icing

>   200 g icing sugar

>   2–3 tbsps boiled, cooled water

Gradually add the water to the icing sugar, beating well until a pouring consistency.

Orange or lemon water icing: Replace the water wi" fresh orange or lemon juice.

Chocolate water icing: Add two tablespoons o' cocoa or drinking chocolate to basic water icing. Also add aboot 25 g o' softened butter and mix wi" hot water rather than cold.

Butter icing (also called buttercream)

Use as a cake coating or a filling or both. Mak' it wi" butter. Dinna mak' it wi" half-fat spreads – ower wattery. And the name is butter icing, no' "sunflooer spread icing".

150–200 g sieved icing sugar

100 g softened butter

Flavouring

The best bit is Licking The bowl

Cream the butter, gradually add the icing sugar and beat until light and creamy. The test for this icing is to be able to taste the sweet before the fat. Add flavourings and/or colourings.

Chocolate butter icing

To the basic add 75 g cooled melted chocolate or 40 g cocoa or chocolate powder mixed wi" 2 tbsps boiling water (allow to cool before adding).

Swiss meringue buttercream

On awfy hot summery days (remember them?) this is no' a cake covering I'd use. It's ower soft. Guid thing we only get aboot fower nice days in a Scottish summer.

  200 g caster sugar

  3 egg whites

  250 g unsalted butter,

     softened but not melted

  1 tsp vanilla extract

Ye'll need a sugar thermometer. Whisk sugar and egg whites wi" a hand whisk in a pan ower simmering water until 60°C is reached.

  Take aff the heat and whisk (wi" an electric mixer) until mixture has doubled in volume and will stand in stiff, glossy peaks.

  Once the bowl is cool, gradually add the softened chopped butter. Beat constantly until the mixture is smooth. It WILL look like it's curdling or losing all its volume. Persevere. Keep beating. It will be ok!

Add the vanilla and mix through. Pipe on cupcakes or use as filling in larger cakes.

Chocolate Swiss meringue buttercream

Melt 150g good chocolate and allow to cool a bit. Add into the buttercream at the end o' the mixing time.

Ganache

Ganache is jist a fancy French name for melted chocolate and cream. It's awfy guid. You can use it when it's still warm tae pour ower cakes and it maks a braw shiny coating, or, wait till it has set, and spread on like buttercream.

Heat 100 g whipping cream till almost boiling. Add to a bowl of 200 g finely chopped dark or milk chocolate, and stir well. Once it's totally melted add 50g softened butter and mix awfy well.

A Simple Way To Ice A Cake

Sift 3 cupfuls icing sugar into a bowl. Separate the whites and yolks of 4 eggs. Put the egg whites on to a large flat plate, add 1 cupful sugar, and beat with a wire whip for 10 minutes. Then add the second cupful sugar with 1 teaspoonful cream of tartar, and continue beating with the same movement.

Add the third cupful sugar, and continue beating with the wire whip until the icing becomes stiff but smooth and fluffy. Then add 1 teaspoonful almond essence, beating it well in. Put the cake to be iced on an icing table or upturned shallow tin, brush off all loose crumbs and even the top

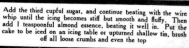

Cover the top and sides of the cake with the icing, using a knife dipped in hot water for the purpose. When the cake is completely covered with a smooth coating set it aside until the icing hardens.

Meanwhile, beat the remaining icing until it is thick enough to retain its shape when pressed through an icing syringe or pastry tube made of glazed white paper. When the foundation icing is firm the cake is ready to be ornamented.

The attractive cake pictured above shows a pretty decoration that is very simple, and yet most effective. A rosette border edges both the top and bottom of the cake, while silver balls, leaves, and lettering give it an unusual finish. These can be bought ready to put on the cake, and give it quite a professional appearance.

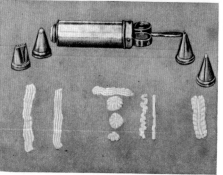

Metal tips to make borders, stems, dots, rosettes, scrolls, and leaves like those shown above can be bought very cheaply, and make decorating a cake at home a simple matter. To make the stems, dots, rosettes, and scrolls the syringe should be held upright, while for borders and leaves it should be held in a slanting position.

Fill the icing syringe with the beaten icing and, holding it in a slightly sloping position, press out the rosette border round the edges of the cake. First of all press out a rosette, then, without lifting the syringe, move it round the cake a little and press out another rosette, making it overlap the first slightly, and continuing until the border is complete.

Ornament the top and sides with rosettes, and while they are still soft press a silver ball in the centre of each. Arrange balls also round the borders. Then decorate with silver leaves and lettering to form any words desired

If coloured icing is preferred, put portions of the icing in different bowls and tint each differently with a good vegetable colour.

Left-over icing will keep for days if it is covered with a damp cloth and put in a cool place.

White chocolate ganache

Heat *100 g* whipping cream. Add *300 g* finely chopped white chocolate. Mix thoroughly.

Royal icing

675 g / 1¼ lb icing sugar, sifted

3 egg whites

3 tsps lemon juice

1½ tsp glycerine

If you're worried about using raw eggs, use egg white powder

Using a paddle beater attachment break up the egg whites till they're a bit frothy. A spoonful at a time, add the icing sugar. Halfway through add the lemon juice and glycerine. Add enough icing sugar tae mak' a mixture that stands up in stiff peaks. To ice a cake (over marzipan) spread on and roughen the surface into peaks. For a smooth surface use a wet pallet knife. You'll need to build a smooth finish up in layers.

How to Decorate a Plain Cake

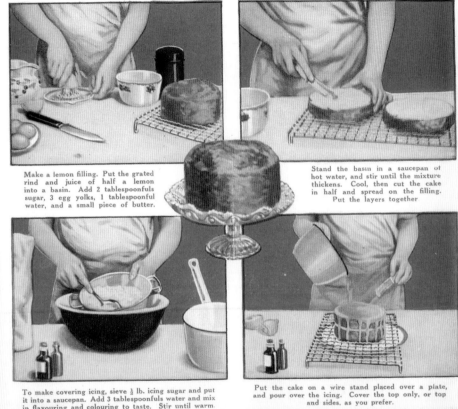

Make a lemon filling. Put the grated rind and juice of half a lemon into a basin. Add 2 tablespoonfuls sugar, 3 egg yolks, 1 tablespoonful water, and a small piece of butter.

Stand the basin in a saucepan of hot water, and stir until the mixture thickens. Cool, then cut the cake in half and spread on the filling. Put the layers together

To make covering icing, sieve ½ lb. icing sugar and put it into a saucepan. Add 3 tablespoonfuls water and mix in flavouring and colouring to taste. Stir until warm.

Put the cake on a wire stand placed over a plate, and pour over the icing. Cover the top only, or top and sides, as you prefer.

Before the icing is properly firmed decorate the cake with pieces of candied orange and lemon peel, arranging them according to taste.

Put any further decorations you fancy on the cake—little silver balls make an effective finish. You now have a real party cake.

Fondant icing (non-cooked version)

   80 g hard white vegetable fat

   100 g glucose syrup

   1 tsp vanilla essence

   $\frac{1}{2}$ tsp salt

   450 g icing sugar

Mix veg fat, glucose, vanilla and salt until smooth. Gradually add the icing sugar and mix until the mixture forms a ball. Wrap wi" cling film and store in an airtight box until you're ready to use.

Marzipan

   250 g icing sugar

   250 g ground almonds

   2 egg whites

   $\frac{1}{2}$ tsp salt

   $\frac{1}{2}$ tsp almond extract

Mix it a' together in a food mixer till it forms a ball. Couldn't be simpler (fingers crossed)!

Easy-To-Make
and
Good-To-Eat

CORNFLOUR CAKE

1 tablespoonful plain	2 oz. butter.
flour.	2 oz. castor sugar.
4 oz. cornflour.	1 teaspoonful baking
2 eggs.	powder

Cream butter and sugar together, break in eggs, work well together. Stir in flour, cornflour, and baking powder, and beat well. Pour into tin, bake in moderate oven for 30 minutes

SPONGE CAKE.

⅛ cupful hot	¾ cupful sugar.
water.	⅞ cupful flour.
1½ teaspoonfuls	¼ teaspoonful salt.
baking powder.	2 eggs.
½ teaspoonful lemon extract.	

Beat eggs, add sugar and hot water Sift flour with salt and baking powder. Add egg mixture, then flavouring, and bake in ungreased tin from 20 to 40 minutes.

VICTORIA SANDWICH.

2 eggs.	1½ teaspoonfuls
1 teacupful sifted	baking powder.
flour.	2 tablespoonfuls
¾ teacupful	milk.
sugar.	

Beat the eggs, add the sugar, and beat for about 10 minutes, then add the flour and milk alternately, and lastly the baking powder. Beat for a few minutes longer, then pour into two fairly large prepared sandwich tins. Ice with lemon icing and decorate with walnuts and cherries.

BRANDY WAFERS.

1 oz butter	1 oz demerara sugar
1 oz flour.	¼ teaspoonful ground ginger
1 oz syrup.	Few drops lemon juice.

Put all in a saucepan except flour. Allow to warm slightly, then stir in flour Put small dessertspoonfuls on greased baking sheet and bake till brown. Cool, remove from tin, and twist round a greased wooden spoon handle When cold and crisp fill with whipped cream

CHERRY MADELINES.

1 teaspoonful baking powder	½ lb flour
3 oz. butter	1 egg
A little milk	

Rub butter into flour, add baking powder, then egg (yolk and white beaten separately), and milk to make a stiff paste Half-fill greased tins with mixture, put a crystallised cherry on each, and bake for 15 minutes

FOR SPECIAL OCCASIONS

1

YULETIDE CAKE.

1. Packed full of goodness is Yuletide Cake! Marzipan covers the top, and there is a layer of chocolate icing decorated with marzipan roses and silver cachous.

2

SIMNEL CAKE.

2. Simnel Cake at Easter or any other time is bound to be a favourite. Marzipan baked to a crusty brown makes the top and the little fruits.

3

NEW YEAR CAKE.

3. This New Year Cake is just right to cut at the festive season. Besides the rich fruit mixture inside there are almonds baked to a crispy golden brown on top.

4

BIRTHDAY CAKE.

4. Birthday Cake is a light mixture with chocolate icing and a posy of fondant flowers on top. The chocolate is roughened with a fork, which gives an attractive appearance.

5

HARVEST CAKE.

5. Harvest cake is a delicious light cake with chopped walnuts through it, a layer of walnut filling, and a good-to-eat outside covering of icing and whole walnuts.

6. Mothers will like Holiday Cake for their children. It is not too rich, and has icing and cherries on top.

Recipes for these cakes appear on page 41.

6

Marzipan Sweets Are Delicious

This is an excellent recipe for marzipan. Sieve 6 oz. icing sugar into a basin, adding it to 8 oz. ground almonds.

Add 1 dessertspoonful rose-water, and mix all together. Then moisten with enough white of egg to bind, kneading well with the hand.

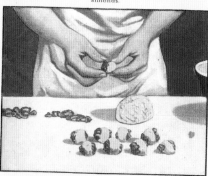

When the marzipan is smooth, form into balls about the size of a walnut. Press a half walnut on each side.

Make some caramel by boiling together 1 lb. loaf sugar, 1 gill water, and a little lemon juice until the mixture is a golden brown colour. Dip the walnuts into this.

Leave to harden, then put in paper cases. These make excellent sweets for parties, and are always popular

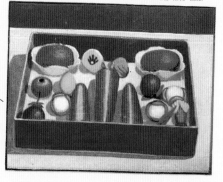

Marzipan can also be made into all sorts of fruits and vegetables with the aid of a little colouring.

Scones,
Teabreads
and Biscuits

Note: In all of these recipes (except wheaten scones), self-raising flour can be used instead of plain with bicarbonate of soda and cream of tartar. And baking powder can be used instead of bicarbonate of soda and cream of tartar to the ratio of 3 level tsps to 200g plain flour.

Scones

Scones are the maist important part o' efteroon tea, no' jist because they're my favourite. They're nicest when they're fresh. Annie, frae oor group, says they freeze well. I've no' tried it as I've never got room in the freezer. Some recipes say "soft but not sticky dough". I say that sticky dough is what you're efter. It maks lighter scones. Just put plenty o' flour on your work surface. Once the liquid is in it, work quickly.

200 g plain flour

50 g sugar (less if preferred)

1 level tsp bicarbonate of soda

2 level tsps cream of tartar

50 g butter or equivalent

1 egg (beaten)

Milk to make up to 125 ml with egg

1 level tsp salt

Preheat the oven to 230°C, 450°F or Gas 8. Sieve dry ingredients. Rub in butter to dry ingredients, add milk mixture, mix to a soft dough. Turn onto a floured surface, work lightly, roll oot to 2 cm thick, cut to size. Place on a floured baking tray. Dust wi" flour or glaze wi" milk an' egg. Bake 8–10 minutes (the scone should sound hollow when its base is tapped). Eat as soon as possible, preferably while still warm. My bairns eat a'thing as soon as possible onyway!

Variations:

For all the variations below follow the basic scone method above.

Cherry scones: As for basic sweet scones but add 50g chopped cherries efter the rubbing-in stage.

Sultana scones: As for basic sweet scones but add 50g sultanas efter the rubbing-in stage.

Date scones: As for basic sweet scones but add 50g chopped dates efter the rubbing-in stage.

Dinna ask Daphne aboot dates!

Cheese scones: Miss oot sugar, halve the butter and add 1 level tsp salt, 100 g grated cheddar cheese, 1 tsp grated parmesan cheese, pinch o' mustard powder.

Herb scones: Using the basic scone mix, leave oot the sugar and add chopped fresh herbs efter the rubbing-in stage.

Citrus scones: Use the grated zest o' 1 orange or lemon per 200g flour.

Others: Desiccated coconut, cocoa, cinnamon, ginger.

Wheaten scones

  150 g wholemeal flour

  50 g plain flour

  1 level tsp bicarbonate of soda

  2 level tsp cream of tartar

  1 level tsp salt

  25 g sugar

  25 g butter

1 egg (beaten)

Milk to make up to 125 ml with egg.

Mix dry ingredients and combine as for basic scones.

Treacle scones

200 g plain flour

25 g sugar

25 g butter

1 level tsp salt

1 level tsp bicarbonate of soda

2 level tsps cream of tartar

1 level tsp cinnamon

1 level tsp mixed spice

1 egg (beaten)

1 tbsp treacle

Milk to mix

Sieve dry ingredients. Rub in butter, add egg, treacle and milk and mix to a soft, sticky dough. Continue as for basic scones.

Attractive Buns for Every day

It is easy to make tea enjoyable when some of these favourite buns are served.

Bath Buns are made with yeast, and are just the thing for tea.

Paris Buns should be sprinkled with sugar and baked in a brisk oven for 20 minutes.

Almond Buns.

8 oz. flour.
2 oz. butter.
1 oz. ground almonds.
2 oz. sweet almonds.
Pinch of salt.
1 heaped teaspoonful baking powder.
2 oz. sugar.
1 egg.
Milk to mix.

Add baking powder and salt to flour and rub in butter. Add almonds, 1 oz. of the sweet almonds (blanched and sliced) and sugar. Beat in well-whisked egg, and add enough milk to make light dough. Form into buns, brush over with milk, press an almond on each, and bake in a hot oven from 10 to 15 minutes.

Barrow Buns.

3 oz. sugar.
1 teaspoonful baking powder.
$\frac{1}{4}$ teaspoonful ground cinnamon.
2 tablespoonfuls grated chocolate.
Chopped almonds.
2 oz. butter.
2 oz. stoned raisins.
2 oz. chopped walnuts.
1 egg.
$\frac{1}{2}$ lb. flour.
Milk.

Sift flour, cinnamon and] baking powder together and rub in butter. Stir in sugar, walnuts, chocolate, chopped raisins, and moisten with well-beaten egg and enough milk to make a soft, dry dough. Form quickly into balls, and place on a lightly-floured tin. Sprinkle chopped almonds on top of each, and bake 20 minutes in a moderate oven.

Bath Buns.

$1\frac{1}{2}$ lb. flour.
$1\frac{1}{2}$ oz. compressed yeast.
Whites of 2 eggs.
Water.
10 oz. sugar nibs.
Yolks of 4 eggs.
8 oz. butter.
Candied peel.
Essence of lemon.

Dissolve yeast in $\frac{1}{2}$ gill tepid water, mix it with eggs and $\frac{1}{4}$ lb. flour. Beat mixture and set before fire to rise. Rub butter into 1 lb. flour, add the sugar, put in peel cut in small cubes. When sponge has risen enough, mix all ingredients together, throw a cloth over it, and set again to rise. Grease a baking tin, form the buns, brush with yolk of egg and milk, and sprinkle with sugar and bake in quick oven for 20 minutes.

Caraway Citron Buns.

5 oz. self-raising flour.
3 oz. castor sugar.
$\frac{1}{2}$ oz. caraway seeds.
4 oz. butter.
2 eggs.
2 tablespoonfuls milk.
2 oz. citron peel.

Beat butter to a cream, add sugar and beat again. Add caraway seeds and citron peel, thinly sliced. Whip eggs well and add to butter and the rest, beating briskly. Continue beating while you add flour and milk. Grease deep patty tins, fill three parts full with batter, and bake in a brisk oven for 15 minutes.

Coffee Buns.

$\frac{1}{2}$ lb. flour.
2 oz. butter.
2 oz. sugar.
1 dessertspoonful coffee essence.
1 egg.
1 teaspoonful baking powder.
Milk.

Sift flour and baking powder and rub in butter. Add sugar, egg, and coffee essence. Moisten to stiff dough with milk. Roll into balls, place in floured baking tin, and brush with beaten egg flavoured with coffee. Sprinkle with sugar, and bake in hot oven.

Before baking Coffee Buns brush them over with beaten egg flavoured with coffee, then sprinkle them with sugar.

Cooky Buns.

$\frac{1}{2}$ lb. flour.
3 oz. sugar.
2 oz. butter.
1 egg (beaten).
1 teaspoonful baking powder.
1 gill milk.

Cream butter and sugar, add remainder of ingredients, roll out, cut in rounds, and bake in a hot oven for 10 minutes.

Farola Buns.

4 oz. Farola.
2 oz. lard and margarine mixed.
2 oz. soft sugar.
2 oz. mixed fruit.
4 oz. flour.
1 teaspoonful baking powder.
1 egg.
Pinch salt.

Place all dry ingredients (except baking powder) in basin. Rub in lard and margarine till fine. Add fruit, baking powder, egg, and, if necessary, milk to mix to stiff dough. Form into balls, brush with egg, and bake in fairly hot oven for 10 to 15 minutes.

Georgia Buns.

$\frac{1}{2}$ cupful butter.
$\frac{1}{2}$ cupful sugar.
3 eggs.
$\frac{3}{4}$ teaspoonful salt.
1 cupful milk.
2 cupfuls flour.
4 teaspoonfuls baking powder.

Cream butter and sugar well, add eggs (beaten well) and milk alternately with the flour, which has been sifted with baking powder and salt. Bake in greased muffin pans for 20 to 25 minutes.

Ginger Buns.

1 lb. flour.
4 oz. butter.
1 oz. chopped preserved ginger.
1 egg.
2 teaspoonfuls baking powder.
2 oz. sugar.
A few drops ginger essence.
A little milk.

Rub butter into flour, add remainder of ingredients (white and yolk of the egg beaten separately) and milk to make a stiff paste. Drop in spoonfuls on well-greased baking sheet and bake.

Ground Rice Buns.

3 oz. flour.
2 oz. butter.
1 teaspoonful baking powder.
3 oz. castor sugar.
3 oz. ground rice.
1 tablespoonful milk.
2 eggs.
1 oz. desiccated cocoanut.

Mix flour, baking powder, ground rice, and cocoanut together. Beat sugar and butter to a cream, add well-beaten eggs gradually, beating all the time. Mix in flour and the rest of the ingredients, a little at a time, and the milk. Beat to a smooth batter and bake in patty pans for 15 minutes. Sprinkle with cocoanut just before baking.

Hot Cross Buns (Without Yeast).

8 oz. flour.
A pinch salt.
2 oz. castor sugar.
3 oz. butter.
2 oz. currants.
1 teaspoonful allspice.
1 teaspoonful baking powder.
2 eggs.
A little milk.
Pastry.

Mix dry ingredients, rub in butter, and add currants. Add eggs (beaten), and milk if necessary. Form into buns, lay pastry crosses on top, and bake for 20 to 30 minutes. While still hot, brush over with a little hot milk and sugar and dry for a moment in the oven.

Hot Cross Buns (With Yeast).

$\frac{1}{2}$ oz. yeast.
Pinch salt.
$\frac{1}{2}$ pint milk.
1 oz. candied peel.
1 teaspoonful ground ginger.
1 lb. flour.
2 oz. butter.
1 teaspoonful mixed spice.
3 dessertspoonfuls sugar.
1 teaspoonful castor sugar (for yeast).

Put yeast into small basin with teaspoonful of sugar and mix till they liquefy. Warm milk and add to yeast. Take half flour and sieve it with salt, and stir in the yeast and milk, and mix all together. Cover the basin loosely and put in warm place for about an hour. Sieve rest of flour with spice and ginger, rub in butter, and add sugar, currants, and peel cut small. Mix all together, and when yeast mixture is ready gradually beat it into it. Turn dough on to a

Muffins

These are braw wi' butter an' this recipe for bramble jam.

200 g plain flour

25 g sugar

1 level tsp bicarbonate
of soda

2 level tsps cream of
tartar

$\frac{1}{2}$ level tsp salt

50 g melted butter or oil

1 egg and milk to mix

Sieve dry ingredients. To these add egg and melted butter or oil, and then add enough milk to mix to an elastic dough. Roll oot to 1 cm thick, cut in rounds. Cook on a heated girdle, till cooked on both sides. Cool in a clean tea towel.

MacDuff's

Nº 24

SCOTTISH FOODS OF QUALITY

Ingredients: 1.5 kg brambles
Water
500 g cooking apples
Sugar

Method:
Wash fruit, cut up apples. Put in preserving pan with water to cover. Simmer till tender and mash well. Strain through scalded jelly bag and allow to drip overnight. Measure the juice and allow 1 kg sugar to each 1250 mls. Heat juice and dissolve sugar in it. Boil rapidly to setting point. Skim, cool and stir before potting in sterilised jars. Cover with circles of greaseproof paper and jar lids while still warm.

Bramble Jam

Scotch Pancakes or Dropped Scones

200 g plain flour

1 level tsp salt

1 level tsp bicarbonate of soda

2 level tsps cream of tartar

25 g sugar

1 dsp golden syrup

1 egg

250ml milk

For Treacle Pancakes replace the syrup with treacle.

Sieve dry ingredients. Add egg, syrup and enough milk tae make a guid thick batter.

Drop spoonfuls o' the mixture onto a fairly hot girdle or non-stick frying pan.

Cook till lightly browned, turn and brown on the ither side. Cool in a clean tea towel.

Crumpets

These are nice enough when they're cold but I think they're better hot. They can be toasted again and served wi" jam and butter.

200 g plain flour

1 level tsp salt

1 level tsp bicarbonate of soda

2 level tsps cream of tartar

25 g sugar

25 g vegetable oil

2 eggs (beaten)

250 ml milk

Why did the doughnut go to the dentist? It needed a filling

Sieve the dry ingredients together. Whisk the eggs and mix wi" the milk. Mix the egg and milk wi" the dry ingredients till smooth, add the oil and mix well. Cook, in spoonfuls o' the desired size (big for Daphnes, wee for bairns), on a hot girdle or non-stick frying pan.

Once cooked on both sides, cool in a clean tea towel.

Doughnuts Are Easy To Make

Half fill a deep saucepan with frying fat and put it on to heat. Line a shallow tin with greased paper and set aside ready for draining. Sift together 3 cupfuls flour, ¾ teaspoonful salt, 1 teaspoonful nutmeg, and 4 teaspoonfuls baking powder.

Cream ⅔ cupful sugar with 3 tablespoonfuls butter, then add 1 beaten egg. Add half of the dry ingredients, then slowly ⅔ cupful milk. Add the rest of the dry ingredients, roll out to ½ inch thick, and cut into rounds with a floured doughnut cutter.

Test the temperature of the hot fat with a small cube of bread. If the bread browns in 60 seconds the fat is just hot enough. Place as many doughnuts in a frying basket as will cover the bottom, and lower it carefully into the fat.

The doughnuts will puff up and rise to the surface of the fat as they cook. When they are brown on one side turn them with a fork and brown them on the other side. They should take 2 minutes to fry.

When they are thoroughly cooked lift the basket out of the saucepan and drain the doughnuts well. Then place them on the prepared lined tin, drain again, and sprinkle with powdered sugar.

If these instructions are followed carefully delicious golden-brown, well-risen doughnuts will be the result. Too hot fat is often the reason for failure, as it causes the doughnuts to crack. Fat that is not hot enough makes greasy doughnuts.

Gipsy Creams

Horace says we should ca' these Romany Creams now. Ah dinna ken much aboot it – but I dinna want tae go offending fowk ower a wee biscuit. Whatever you ca' them, this recipe is braw.

50 g butter and 50 g cooking fat

75 g caster sugar

1 dsp syrup

2 dsps hot water

100 g rolled oats

100 g self-raising flour

$\frac{1}{2}$ tsp baking soda

Few drops vanilla essence

Cream fats and sugar, add syrup melted in water, then add ither ingredients. Make into wee balls and bake at 190°C (375°F, Gas 5) for aboot 15 minutes or until golden broon. When cold, sandwich wi' chocolate butter icing (page 137).

Oaty Biscuits

We a' ken oats are guid for ye, an' I like ma porridge richt enough, but oats dinna taste much nicer than when they're in these wee beauties. These oaty biscuits have been a favourite in oor hoose for as long as I can remember and I came across the source the ither day! From _The Galloway News Cookery Book_ o' 1954 and submitted by Mrs McSherry from Auchencairn. Thank you Mrs McSherry!

125 g butter and 75 g lard

1 tbsp golden syrup

2 tbsps water

3 cups (250 g) porridge oats

1 cup (130 g) self-raising flour

1 tsp baking soda

1 cup (200 g) sugar

Melt together the butter, lard, syrup and water. Mix the dry ingredients together and add the melted mixture. Mix well. Put in teaspoonfuls on a greased baking tray allowing room to spread.

Bake at 190°C (375°F, Gas 5) till broon.

Allow to cool on the baking tray before removing to an airtight box.

Palmiers

Palmiers in French, Palmeras in Spanish, Schweineohren in German, Elephant Ears in oor hoose. Betty Pringle brought them back frae Torremolinos, she didnae ken they were so easy tae make! These are awfy nice wi" a wee cuppa, and one is no' enough. And the Spanish hae them for breakfast wi" hot chocolate. I quite fancy that but Paw likes his sassidges. Twa sandwiched together wi" cream in the middle is just braw! This is the very dab for using up your pastry scraps – it always seems tae mak' just enough! And it's richt easy tae mak' these intae savoury palmiers. Sprinkle wi" a bit o' hard cheese, or some herbs on the pastry before you roll them up.

Roll oot your puff pastry (pages 72–76) into a rectangle that is just 3 mm thick. Sprinkle evenly wi" sugar (a sugar sifter is useful). Press it doon.

Roll up both long edges o' the pastry towards each other tae meet in the middle.

Brush a wee bitty egg or water doon the middle to stick the two halves together.

Chill for 30 minutes then, using an awfy sharp knife, cut into 5 mm/¼ inch slices.

Put on a baking tray covered in baking parchment, brush wi" beaten egg, then bake at 200°C (400°F, Gas 6) for 10–15 minutes or until broon.

Custard Creams

75 g butter

75 g plain flour

25 g icing sugar

25 g custard powder

Cream the butter and sugar together, mix in the flour and custard powder. Roll into balls and flatten slightly wi' a fork. Bake at 190°C (375°F, Gas 5) till pale broon. Sandwich together wi' butter icing (page 137).

Ginger Shortcake

Shortcake

100 g butter

50 g caster sugar

125 g plain flour

1 level tsp baking powder

1 level tsp ground ginger

Topping

4 level tbsps icing sugar

50 g butter

1 level tsp ground ginger

3 level tsps syrup

Cream butter and sugar. Mix in dry ingredients. Spread mixture into a 20-cm/8-inch greased tin. Bake at 180°C (350°F, Gas 4) for 40 minutes. Melt the topping ingredients together. Pour ower the shortcake once cooked. When topping has set, cut into wedges.

Shortbread

Ye cannae hae a Scottish spread withoot shortbread and everyone has aye got their ain version. I've never eaten a variation that I didnae like. I like this rice-flour version, it gies it a braw flavour and crunch. Cut them intae wee dainty fingers for efternoon tea (then ye can hae twa at a time).

150 g plain flour and 50 g rice flour
100 g butter
50 g caster sugar

Mix flour and sugar. Work in the butter using the hands. Knead well, shape into cakes using a mould, or press into a baking tray, or roll into strips (dinna roll it ower thin!). Prick it wi' a fork, put individual biscuits on baking tray, and bake at 170°C (330°F, Gas 3) for 30–40 minutes until pale broon. Cut afore it gets cold.

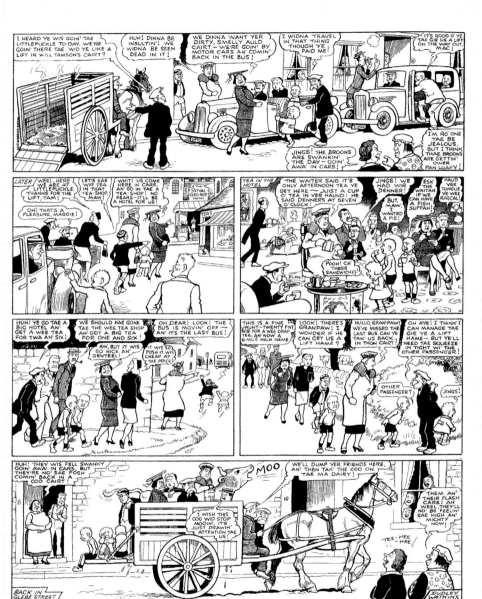

Empire Biscuits

Here's anither sweet thing that had a name change because o' the war. Before World War I they were ca'd "Linzer Biscuits" and "German Biscuits". When war broke oot, they (ah'm no entirely sure who "they" were, the Ministry o' Biscuits maybe?) changed it tae Empire Biscuits.

150 g butter

250 g plain flour

75 g caster sugar

1 egg

1 tsp baking powder

Cream butter and sugar together. Then add the egg and other ingredients. Knead well and roll oot thinly, cut in roonds. Bake at 200°C (400°F, Gas 6) for 10–12 minutes or until cooked. Cool. Sandwich together wi" seedless raspberry jam. Ice the tops wi" water icing (page 136) and decorate wi" a wee glacé cherry.

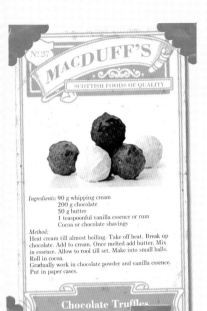

Ingredients: 90 g whipping cream
200 g chocolate
50 g butter
1 teaspoonful vanilla essence or rum
Cocoa or chocolate shavings

Method:
Heat cream till almost boiling. Take off heat. Break up chocolate. Add to cream. Once melted add butter. Mix in essence. Allow to cool till set. Make into small balls. Roll in cocoa.
Gradually work in chocolate powder and vanilla essence. Put in paper cases.

Chocolate Truffles

Ingredients: 500 g granulated sugar
1 tablespoonful golden syrup
50 g butter
Vanilla essence
250 ml evaporated milk

Method:
Heat milk and syrup in a pan. Add sugar and butter. Stir to dissolve sugar. Bring slowly to boiling point. Bring to 118°C stirring all the time. Remove from heat, add vanilla. Beat till beginning to grain. Pour into greased tin and allow to cool. Cut into fingers when cold.

Vanilla Tablet

Ingredients: 1 kg raspberries
1 kg sugar

Method:
Put fruit in preserving pan and warm till juice flows. Mash well. Simmer till fruit is soft and well broken. Add sugar and stir till it has dissolved. Increase the heat and bring to the boil. Boil till it reaches setting point. Skim, cool and stir before potting in sterilised jars. Cover with circles of greaseproof paper and jar lids while still warm.

Raspberry Jam

Index

Published 2013 by Waverley Books, an imprint of
DC Thomson Books Group Ltd,
144 Port Dundas Road, Glasgow, G4 0HZ

Maw Broon is Copyright © and
Registered ® 2013, DC Thomson & Co Ltd

www.dcthomson.co.uk

Recipes supplied by Gilda T Smith

Other text by Waverley Books

Copyright © 2013, DC Thomson Books Group Ltd.

Oaty Biscuits courtesy of and © The Galloway News,
published with kind permission

Picture Credits

A catalogue entry for this book is available from the British Library

ISBN 978-1-84934-328-2

32036

Printed and bound in China

Typeset in Bowen Script

Ingredients	Spoons
Flour, Cornflour, Custard Powder	25 g = 3 level 15 ml tbsps
Cheese (grated)	25 g = 4 level 15 ml tbsps
Breadcrumbs	25 g = 6 level 15 ml tbsps
Sugar	25 g = 2 level 15 ml tbsps
Rice (uncooked)	25 g = 2 level 15 ml tbsps
Gelatine	10 g = 3 level 5 ml tsps

UK Liquid Measures			
Unit	Equals (approx.)	UK fluid ounces/pints	Millilitres
1 teaspoon	1/3 tbsp	1/5 fl oz	5 ml
1 dessertspoon	2 tsps	2/5 fl oz	10 ml
1 tablespoon	3 tsps	3/5 fl oz	15 ml
1 cup	16 tbsps	1/2 pint	285 ml
1 UK fluid ounce	2 tbsps	1/20 pint	28 ml
1 UK pint	2 cups	20 fl oz	570 ml
1 gill	1/4 pint	5 fl oz	140 ml
1 quart	2 pints	40 fl oz	1136 ml
1/2 UK pint	1 cup	10 fl oz	285 ml
1/4 UK pint	1/2 cup	5 fl oz	115 ml
2 UK pints	1 quart	40 fl oz	1136 ml
1 litre	4 1/2 cups	scant 2 pints	1000 ml
1 UK gallon	4 quarts	8 pints	4560 ml

UK/Metric	US Measures		
3.79 litre (4 litres)	1 gallon	16 cups	4 quarts
0.95 litre (1 litre)	1 quart	4 cups	2 pints
450 ml (500 ml)	1 pint	2 cups	16 fl oz
240 ml (250 ml)	1/2 pint	1 cup	8 fl oz
120 ml (125 ml)	1/4 pint	1/2 cup	4 fl oz
25 ml (30 ml)	1/16 pint	2 tbsps	1 fl oz
15 ml =1 UK tbsp	roughly the same as a US tablespoon		
5 ml =1 UK tsp	roughly the same as a US teaspoon		
1 UK cup = 285 ml	1 US cup plus 2–3 tablespoons approx.		